DAda POP

the persistence of memory by image

by

Natascia Gec

Index

1. The avant-guarde : the origins

Dada and Pop Art originated in a different way of seeing the world . Both were pacifistic movements reacting against the imbecility of the war either WWI or Korea and Vietnam , both were movements playing with the philosophy of "Epater les bourgeois" meaning making humour out of the prudery and jokes about sexual inhibitions of the lowest middle class by challenging the everyman doing unusual things or watching pictures and sculptures with unusual eyes , both by inventing , imagining and suggesting an innovative perspective of keeping memory of even everyday life moments and let them persist on the retina by the image chosen. Both used black and white and lively colours , both used new techniques in photography and both were not so arrogant not to acknowledge they had common origins in art , great masters to copy and follow though from a different perspective and to self copy one the other without fearing of being too boastful. They were self ascertained of their own value and relentless to give up on art.

They start from the impression , as Claude Monet stated :"In my opinion the landscape does not exist because its aspect changes every moment , nut the surrounding atmosphere revives it – the air and light that are ever changing . It is only the surrounding atmosphere that give value to the object." He was discussing the prevalent idea in history of art of a fixed correspondence between object and colour which in science it is called perceptive constance . Furthermore he introduced the serie , like the Cathedral of Rouen , The British Parliament , the nympheas and other subjects , with same topic and different colour with coloured shadows . A theme furhter explored by both Dada in photography and Pop Artists.

From the post impressionist like Cezanne they symplified forms and metamorphosed them into other things , in a geometrical sense or deforming them to give the emotion of the artist as in expressionism .

As Medardo Rosso stated upon his art :" There is nothing material , we ourselves are only shadows of light ".

Together with violent pincelling and lively colours in expressionism came out another parallel current , divisionism which divided the colour in stains more or less geometrical like Paul Gauguin , Lega Segantini and Fattori , or Pelizza da Volpedo (Macchiaioli) , up to points (Pointillisme) by Seurat and Signac among others. Vincent Van Gogh would choose the spiral.

From Henri de Toulouse Lautrec they took the grotesque mask , the deforming mirrors of the Music Hall or Circus, the dissolute humanity which peopled the streets and the use of xilography and posters for commercials.

Then another avant-guarde origin is Symbolism with the Manifesto by Jean Moreas in 1886 the year of the last exhibition by the Impressionist and its being enemies of the positivist rationality , in fact at the turn of the century Einstein introduced the concept of relativism (1905/10/21) , and the dressing of the idea into a sensible form hiding in dreams , imagination , fantastic , myths and history , in the cult of beauty , but with a morbid , sensual connotation , almost decadent ,as introduced by Sigmund Freud in his "Interpretation of Dreams"1901. Thus in Pierre Puvis de Chavannes , Gustave Moreau , Arnold Boecklin , Odilon Redon and the Pre-Raphaelites.

The birth of photography started the exploration of new possibilities in art for both generations , Dada and Pop Artists.

From this last period of the nineteenth century (1874/1886) they took also the fashion of Nipponism , with symbols and clothing or landscapes from Japan .

The Polynesian isles and Africa came into the fashion for exotic paintings and sculptures through Paul Gauguin , the fauves and Matisse . From here started Primitivism and Cubism .

Futurism was researching the movement into the static art , while abstractism took inside biology and other sciences .

Finally Metaphysical art returned to a clash between the new factory reality and the ancient history of symbolism in art.

The sensuality and morbidity is there to "epater les bourgeois".

Impressionism

Claude Monet is the great master of series en plein air

We recognize the Cathedral of Rouen then reproduced also by a new technique by Roy Lichtenstein

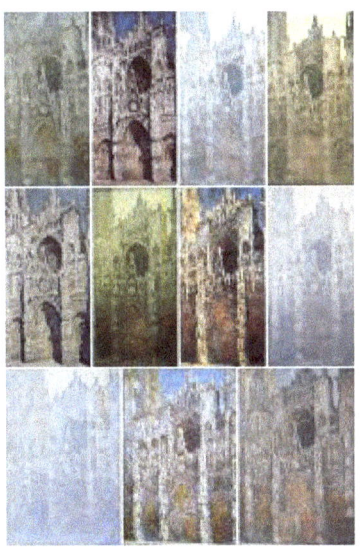 Monet

Roy Lichtenstein

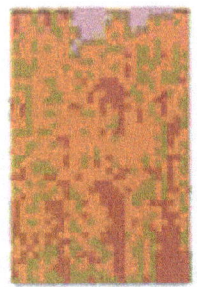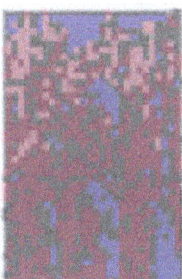

We recognize his famous
Straw sheaves

Claude Monet

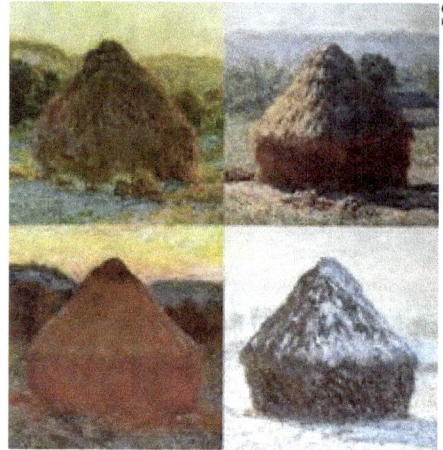

Roy Lichtenstein

And his nympheas at Giverny

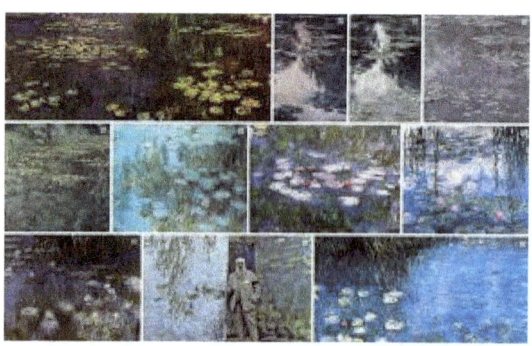

Roy Lichtenstein

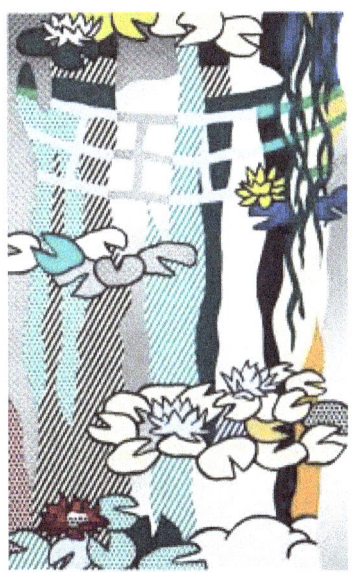

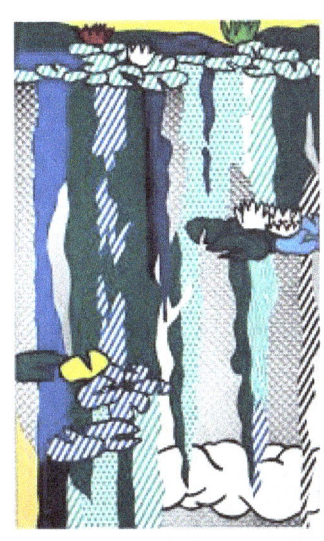

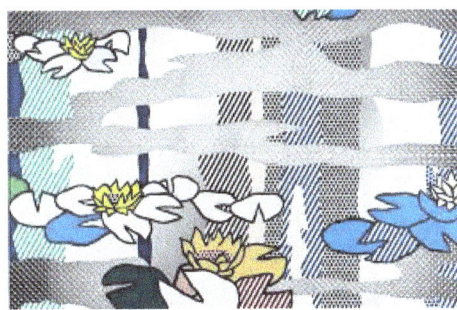

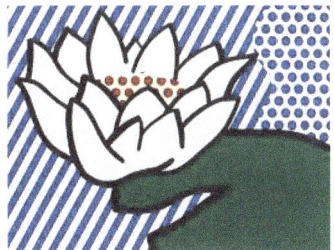

Nympheas were inspiring also for the Dada

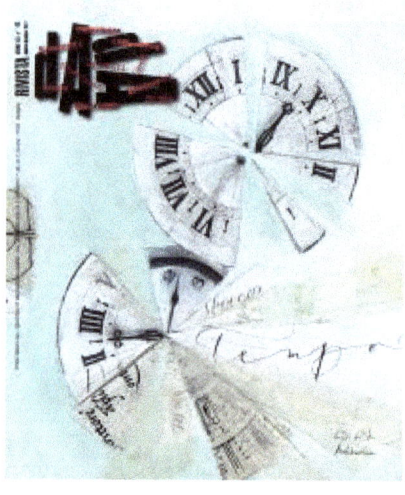

transformed into something new the time elapsing and flourishing .

Each painter was inspired by different masters of impressionism in Surrealism

Rene` Magritte reinvented the Balcony of Eduard Manet

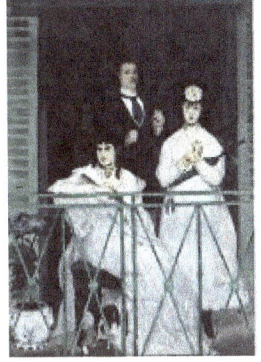 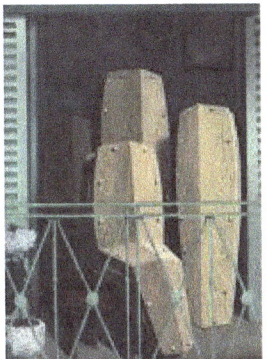

While Salvador Dali` reinvented the L`angelus by Millet

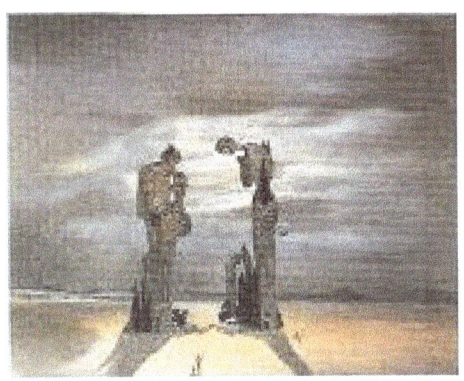

Dali`

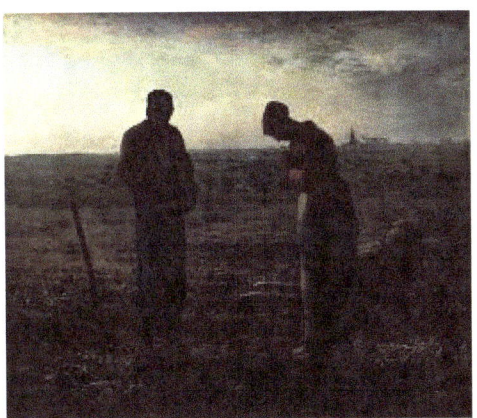

Millet

Paris was the centre of the world during the years 70s and in 1889 when the Universal Exposition saw for the first time the shape of the Tour Eiffel .

The most loved Icon was the Mona Lisa or Gioconda by Leonardo da Vinci which is exposed in the Louvre Museum.

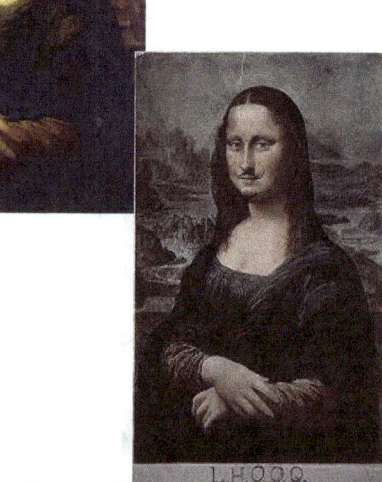

The small portrait was reinvented by Marcel Duchamp with moustaches and goatie and the inscription at the base Elle a les quais au cul which means more or less "she is annoyed"

The Impressionists reinvented it in the Lise By Auguste Renoir actualising the woman but not the pose

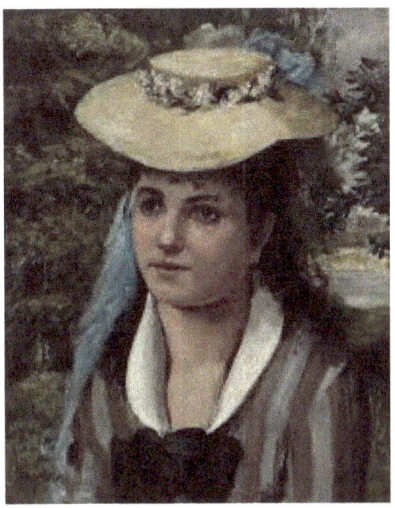

Rene` Magritte reinvented it in a new key

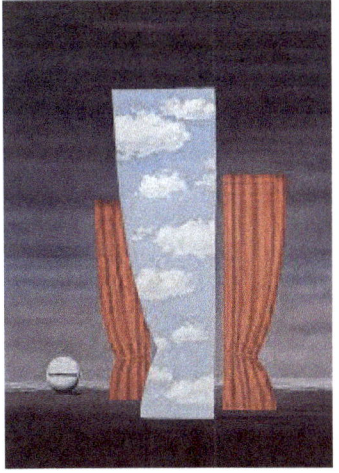

The Pop Artists were inspired especially Andy Warhol

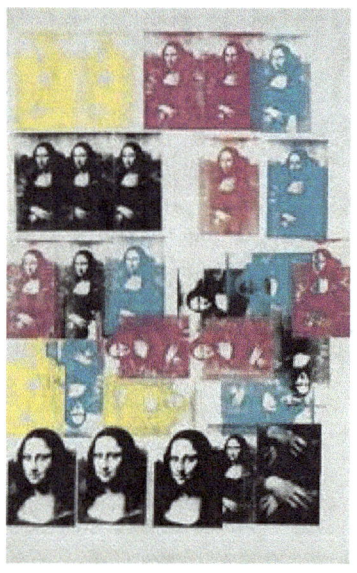

and Roy Lichtenstein

"and then I`ll just sit here and smile "

Expressionism

The two masters of expressionism that were most inspirational were Vincent Van Gogh and Edvard Munch

The former copied from the Impressionists the sheaves adding labour and people

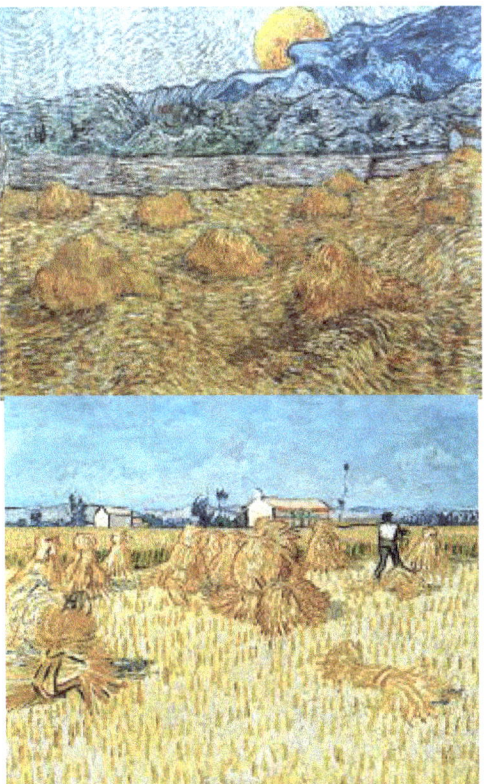

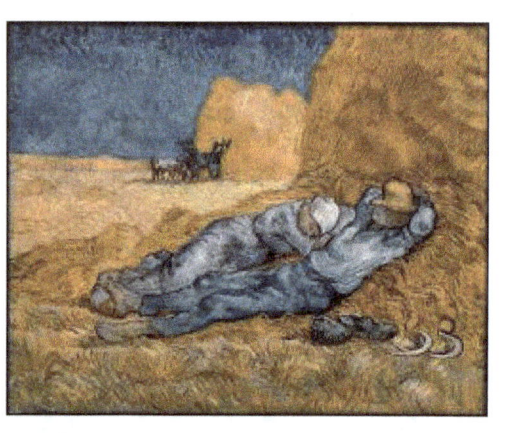

The latter giving a new meaning to women seen as tri-
dimensional , mother , daughter
and lover in his Madonna serie

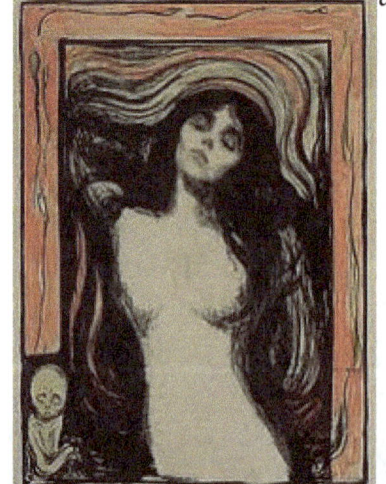

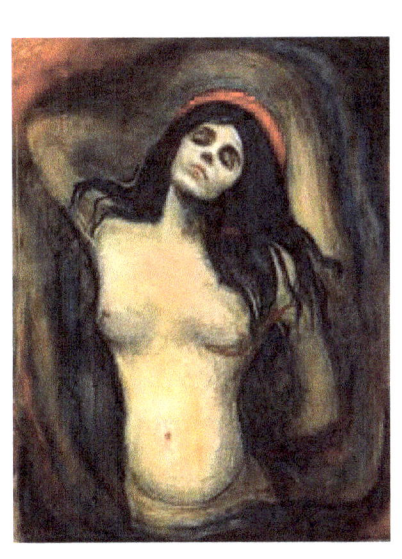

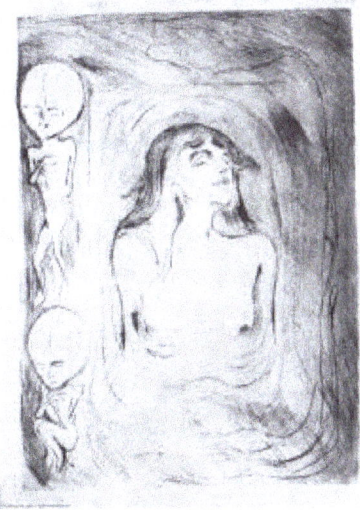

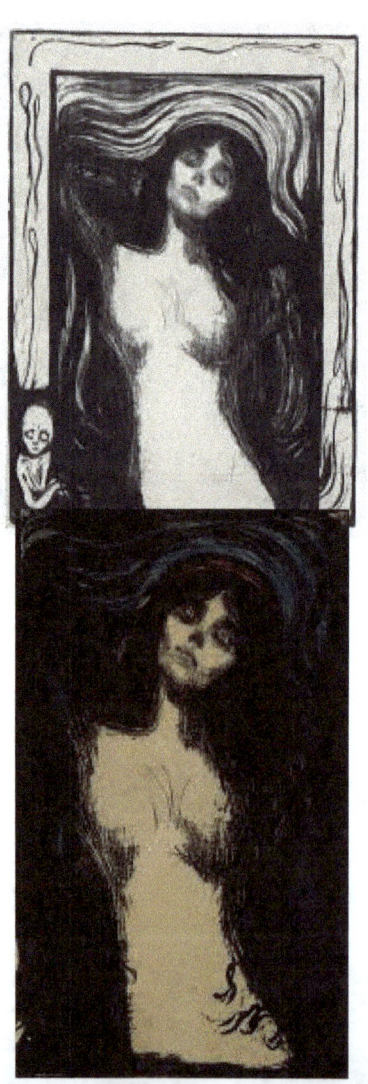

Ri-elaborated by Andy Warhol in his series about Munch

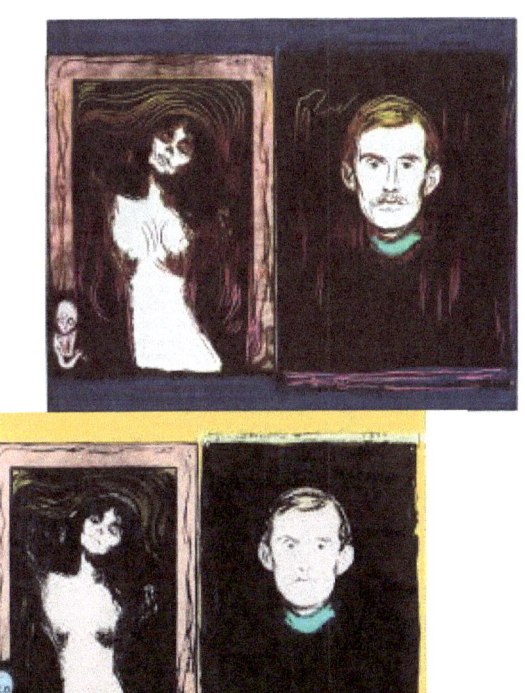

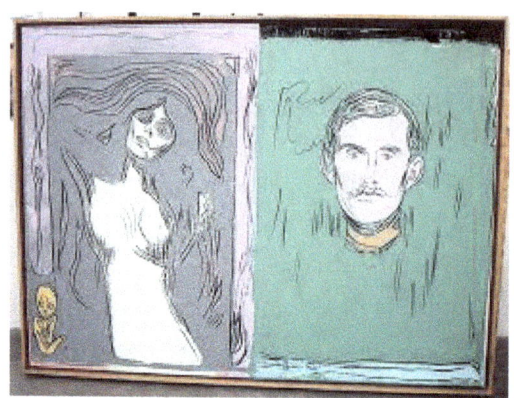

Divisionism

Divisionism is dividing the colour in atoms from the macro stain to the minimal point . The New technique was well accepted both by Surrealism and Pop Art

Besides the use of white on white to give special effects already started by Whistler , in this period becomes the vague

to describe animals , landscapes and people .

Black and white photos and paintings originated in divisionism

Whistler

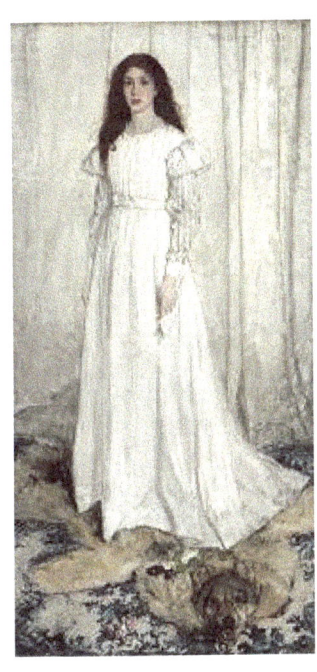

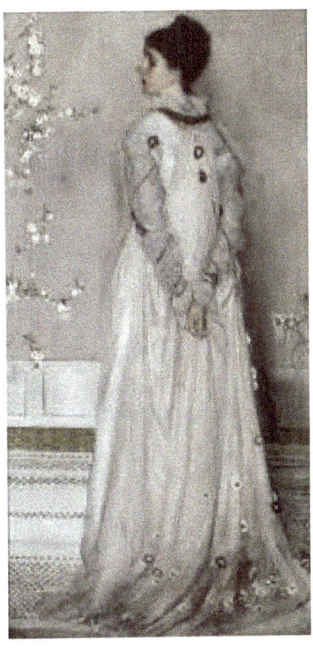

Whistler

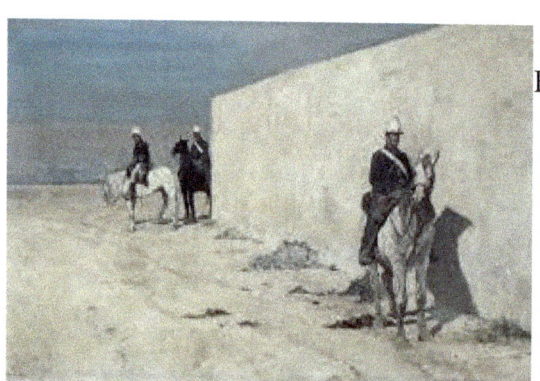

Fattori

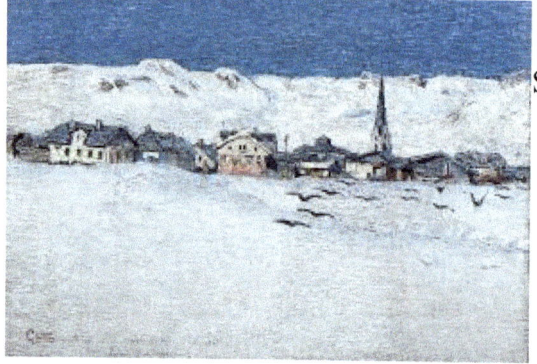

Segantini

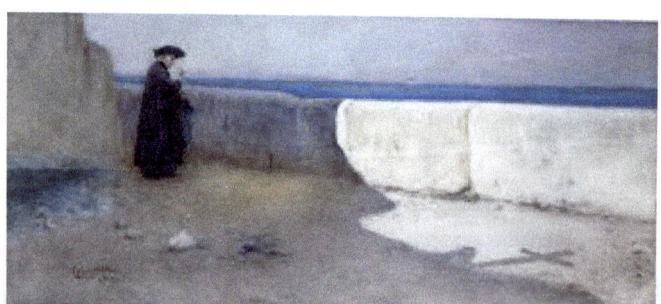

Lega

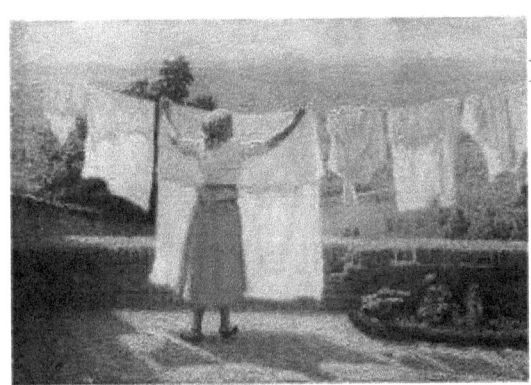

Morbelli

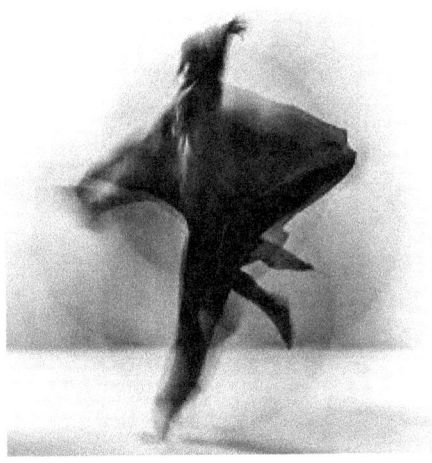

Man Ray

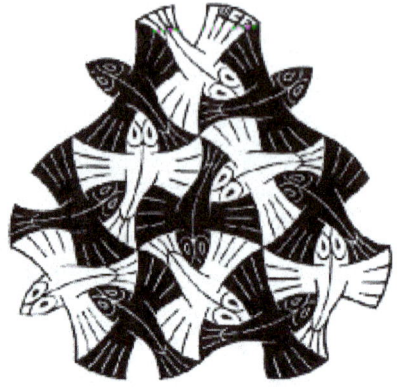

Escher
Maurits

Roy Lichtenstein

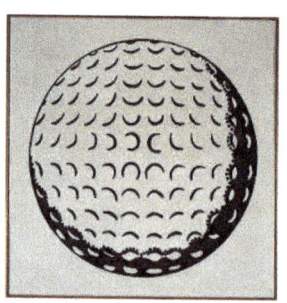

The division in small points give a new perspective on light and the atom with the new theories of Rutherford at the beginning of the twentieth century

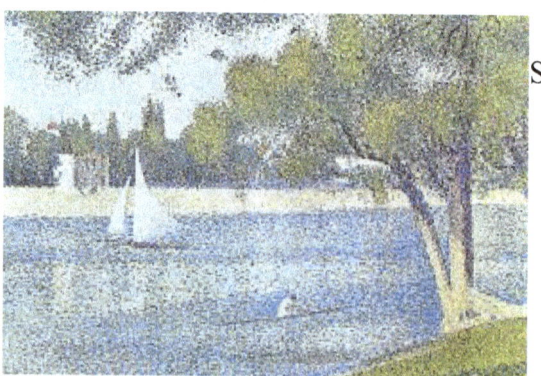

Seurat

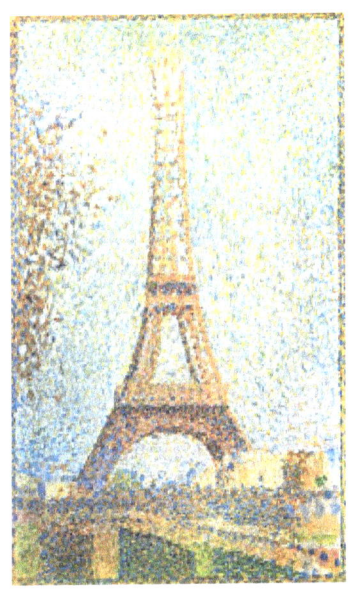

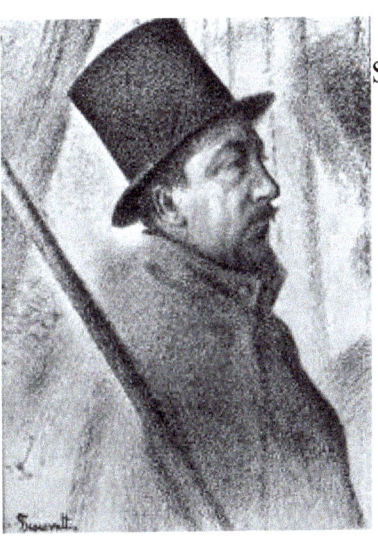

Signac

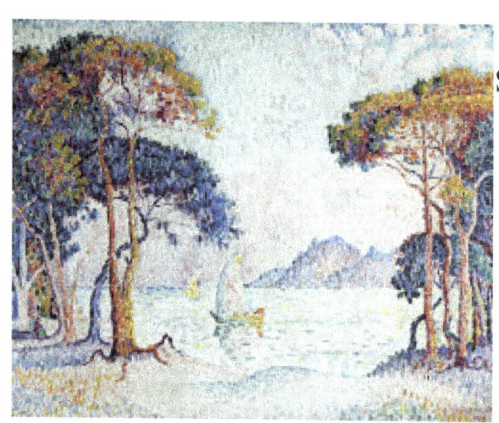 Signac

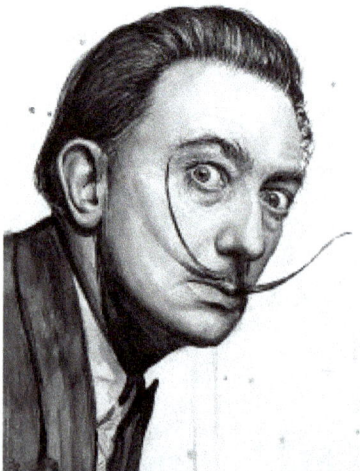 Dali the author is reflecting a pose and creating an image

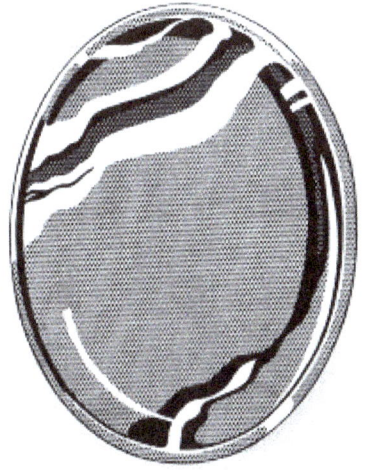

Roy Lichtenstein

The mirror is not reflecting the author but the image itself/

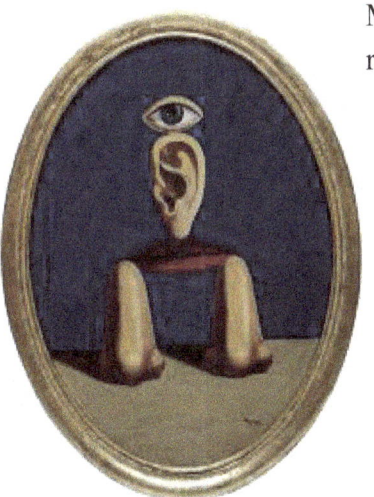

Magritte The run of white

Here the image is reflecting only singular parts of the author.

Here the author is tangled to the past

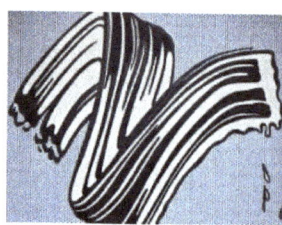

or free to create Toy Lichtenstein

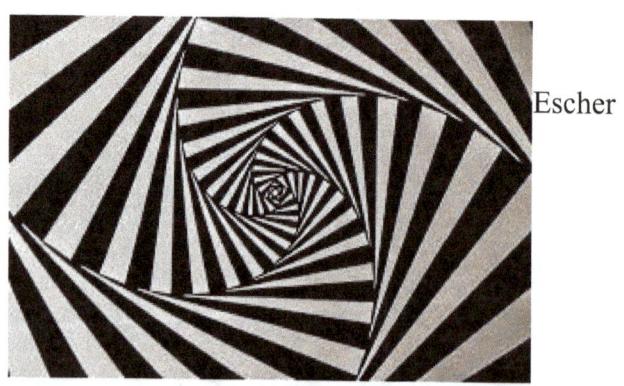

Escher

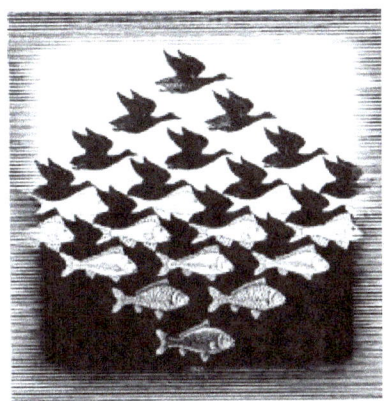

Escher

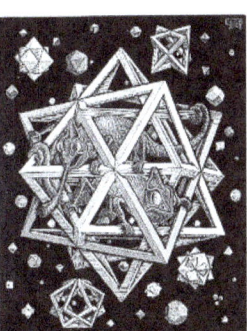

The atom is part of
the painting

Escher

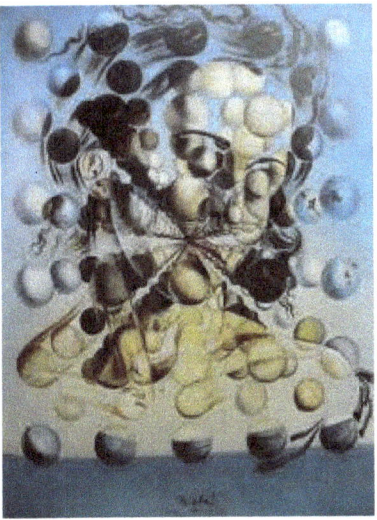

Dali Galatea

Magritte
selt
portrait.

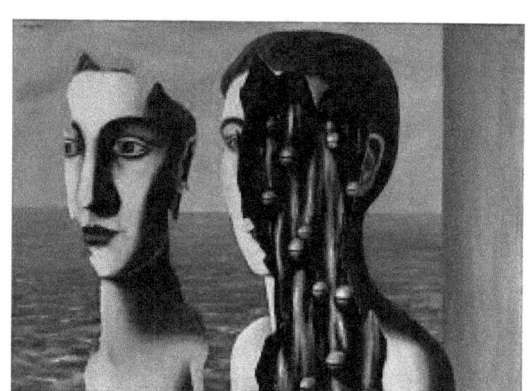

Symbolism

After and in contemporary years the Dada created each
different symbols

Hans Arp the omphalos

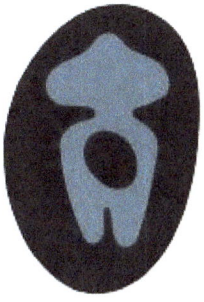

And the turtle flying in his Peace collage

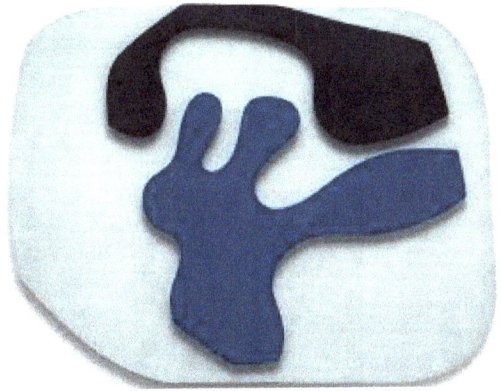

Max Ernst was haunted by his bird reminiscing the sphinx by Gustave Moreau

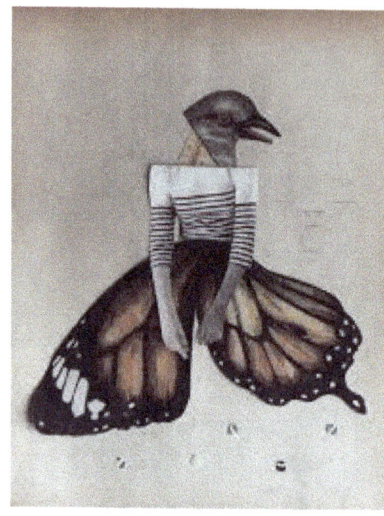

the moth is
symbol of the
time passing
like in the poem
by Dorothy
Parker

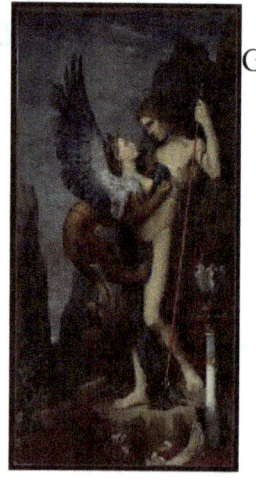

Gustave Moreau

Max Ernst Le Romantisme

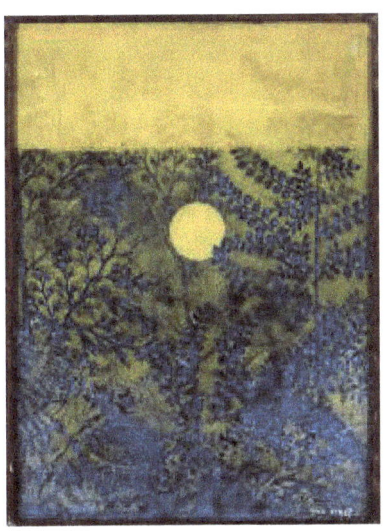

time and colour remind of the fauves and the expressionism though the historical period of Romanticism is typical of Symbolism.

Marcel Duchamp was keen on the chessboard of which he became a professional player

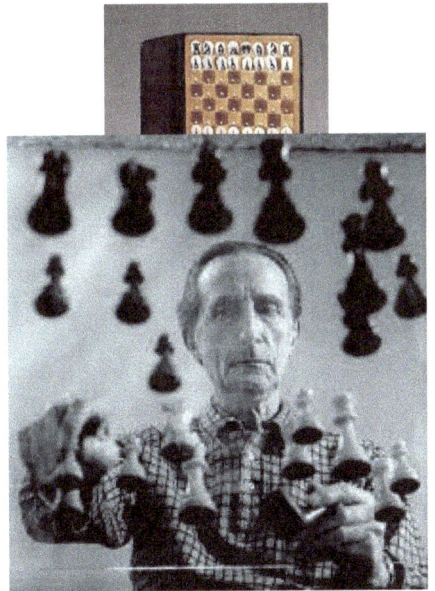

Marcel Duchamp

Then another symbol of Dada in general is time and staircases

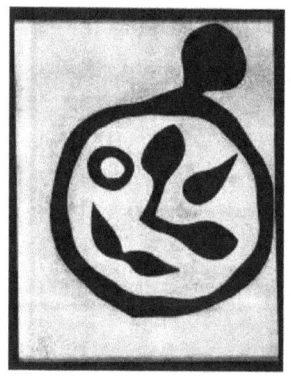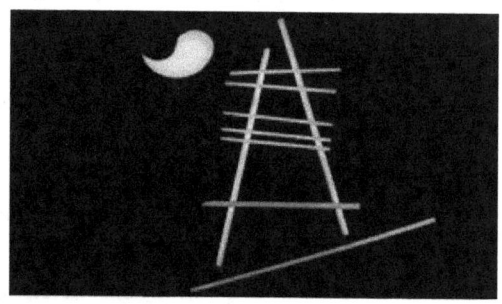

Hans Arp   Marcel Duchamp

Surrealists like Magritte invented the man in a bowler , clouds ,
the apple , the masks and the pipe

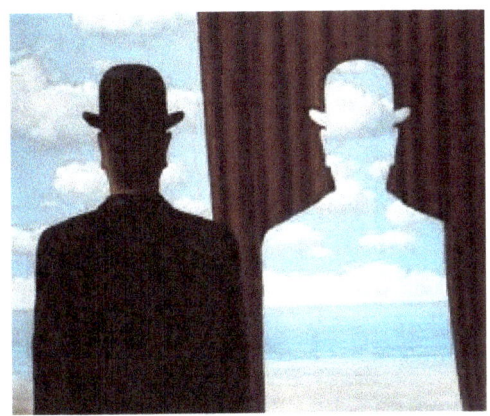

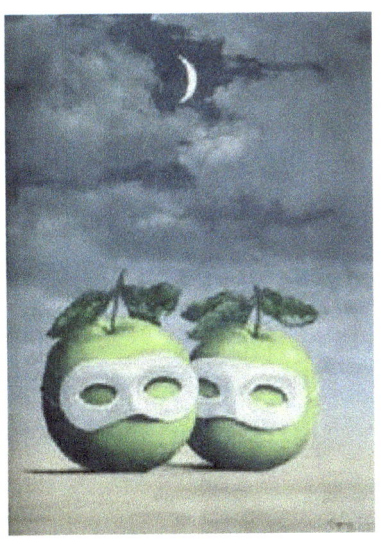

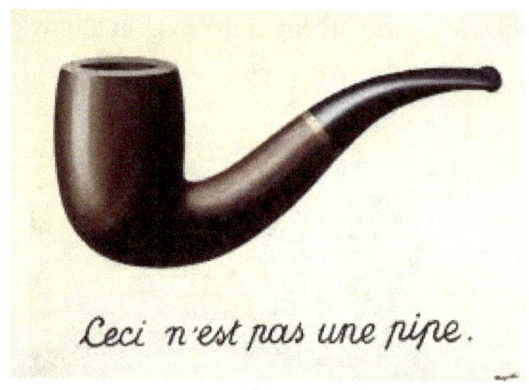

Ceci n'est pas une pipe.

the turtle symbol of people is resumed

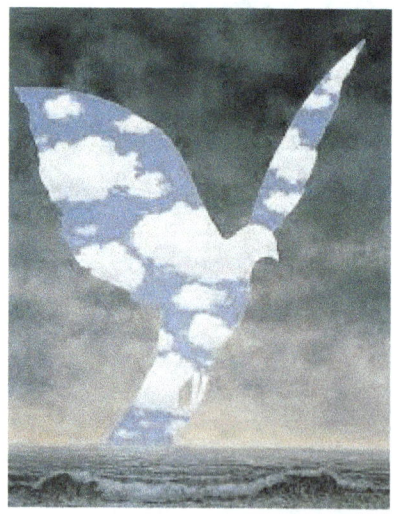

Dali` experimented with ants , elephants , swans , bread and biccycles , and time of which he was addicted

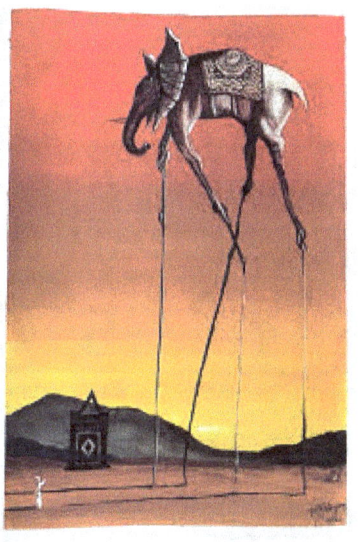

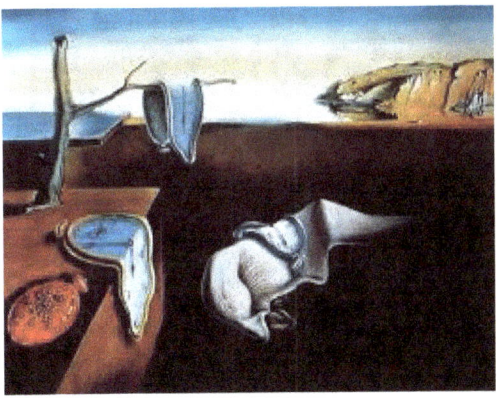

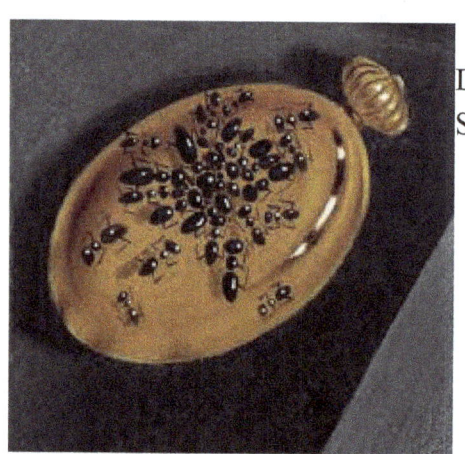

Dali`
Salvador

Escher resuggested the staircase motive

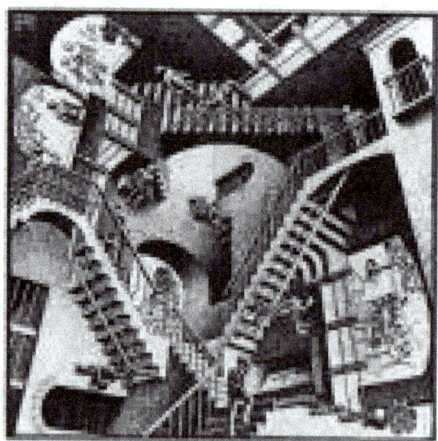

Warhol in pop art has decided for the iconic Campbell soup can

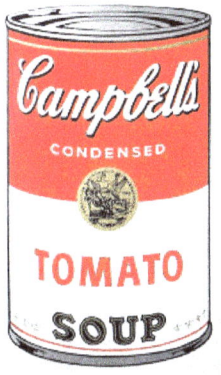

Lichtenstein among the paint brush , the mirrors , the blonde and the brunette has also music notes

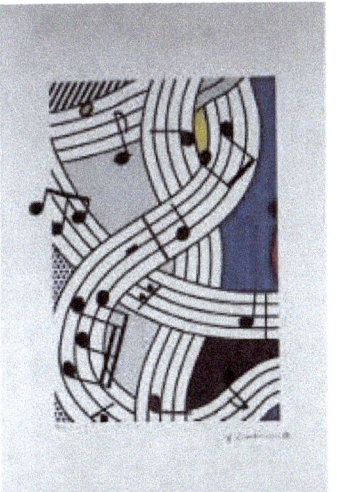

Oldenburg has the ice-cream

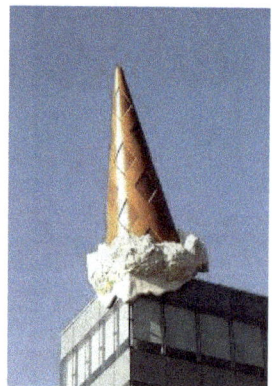

While Rauschenberg has the umbrellas reminiscent of the Pre-Raphaelites The last of England

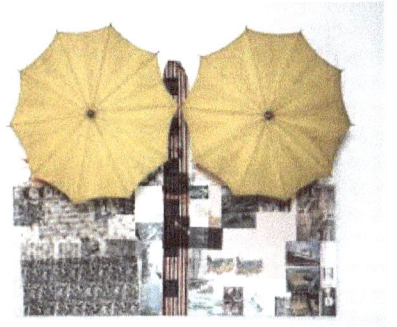
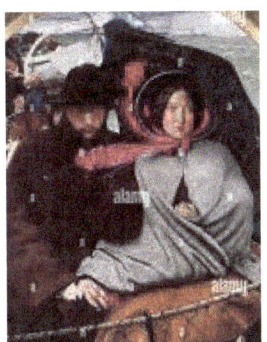

and the scapegoat reminiscing Millais one

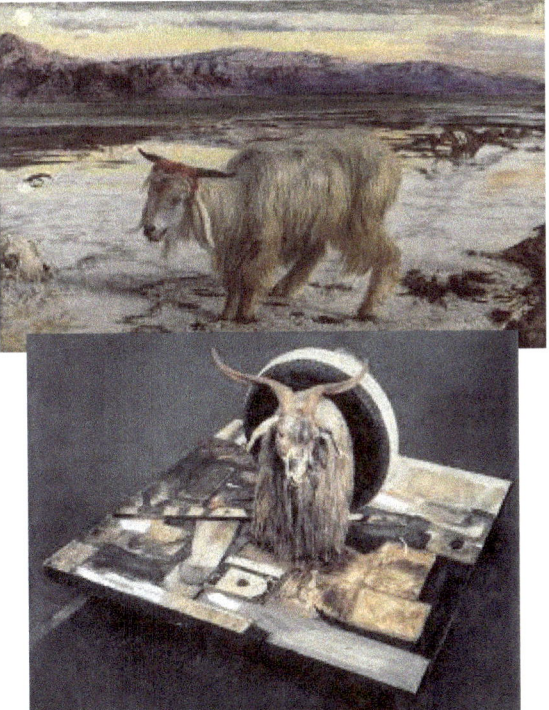

Robert Rauschenberg

or Roy Lichtenstein reminiscing Arnold Bocklin`s the Secret Isle

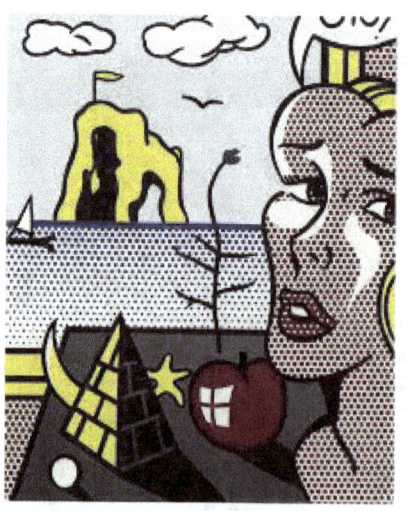

Arnold Bocklin

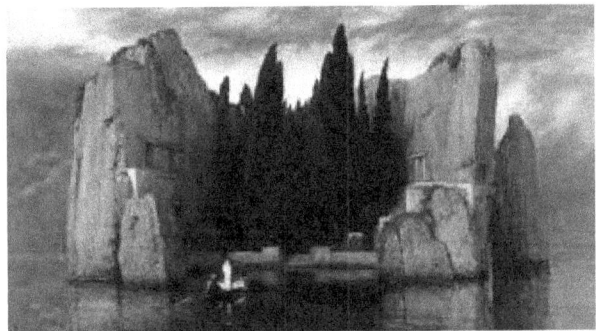

Cubism

From Cubism (1908) they took the idea of tridimensionality in contemporaneity and the primitivism of Africa , the idea of a research for movement already in Matisse Henri and the concept of pacificism with the refusal of war as violence not only from the physical but also from the intellectual point of view.

Pablo Picasso , Georges Braques and Constantin Brancusi were the most influential on Dada and Pop artists .

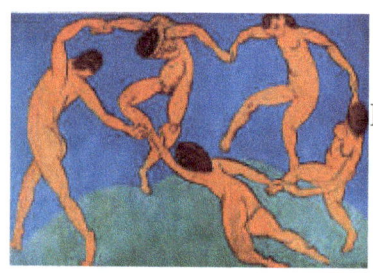

Henri Matisse
Dancing

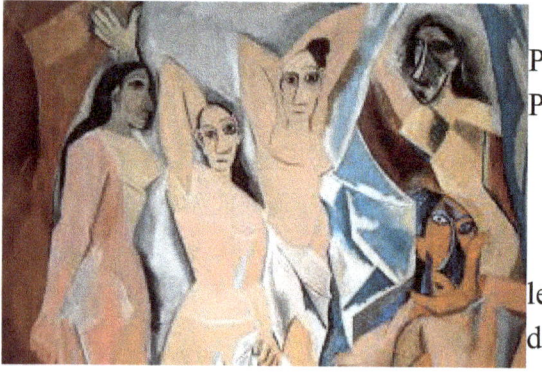

Pablo
Picasso

les
demoisell
es

d`Avignon

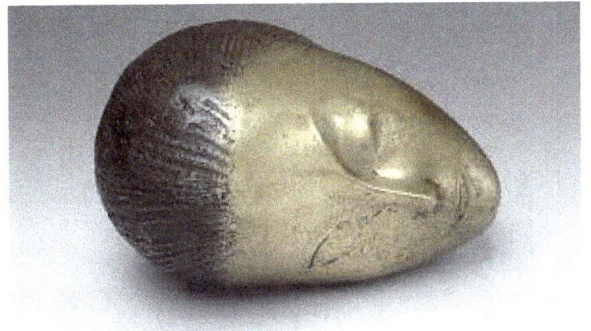

Constantin Brancusi muse

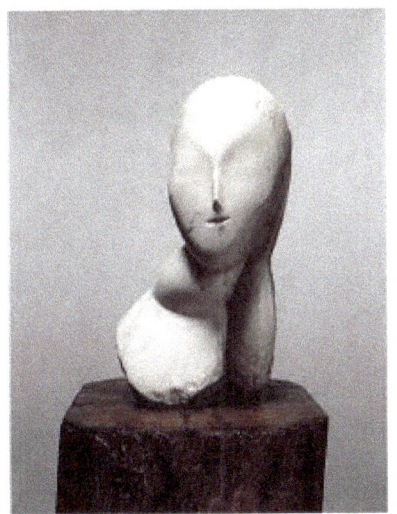

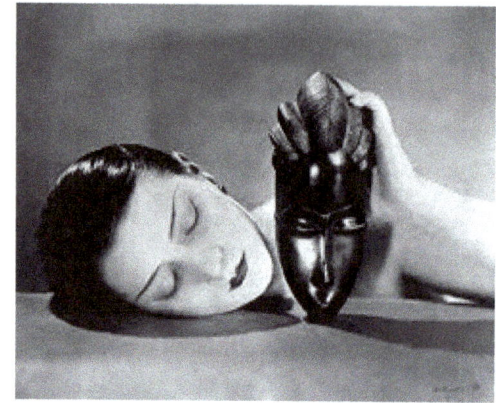

Man Ray
Lee Miller

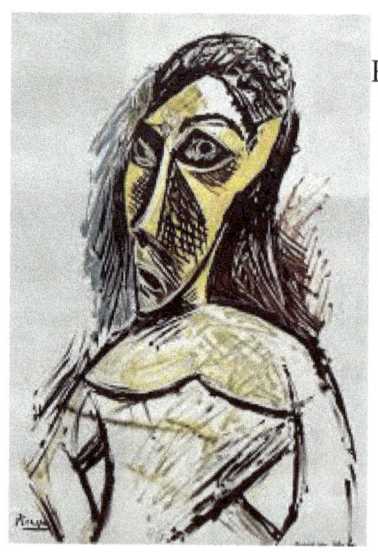

Pablo Picasso

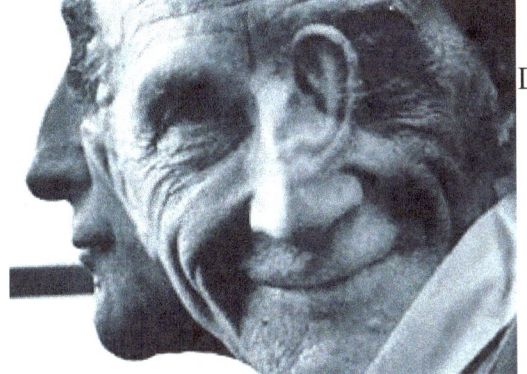

Man Ray

Duchamp

Pablo Picasso

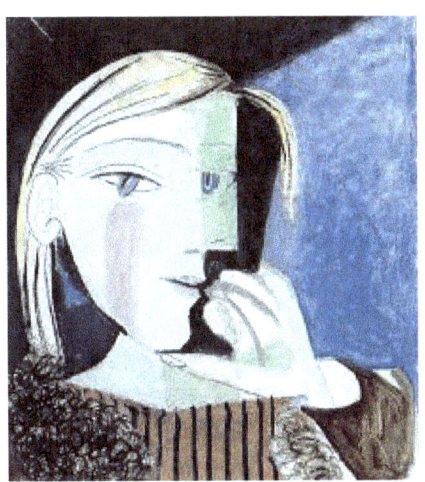

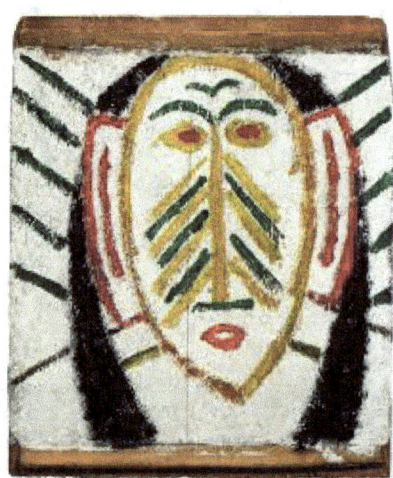

Pablo Picasso

Munari Dada Pop

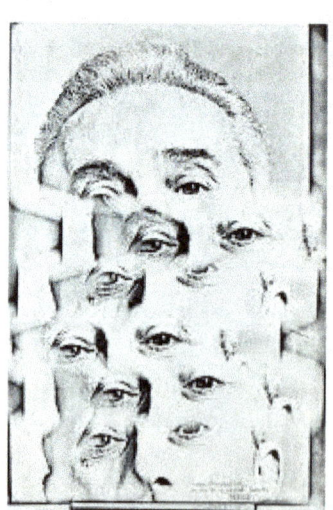

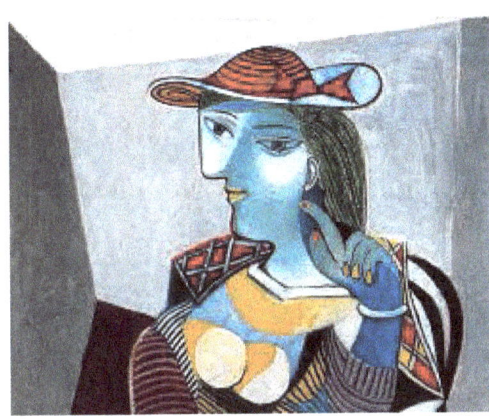

Pablo
Picasso

Jean Michel Basquiat

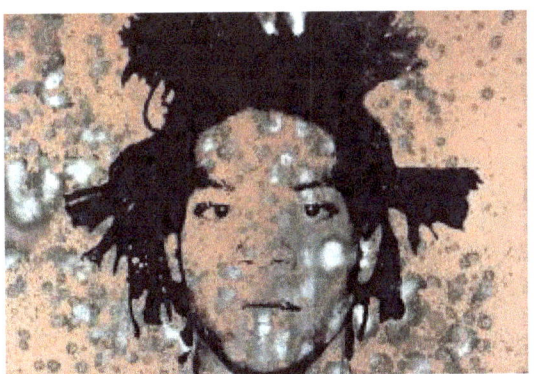

From this sequence of Roy Lichtenstein we pass from the realistic Picassian bull to cubism abstractism and Pop.

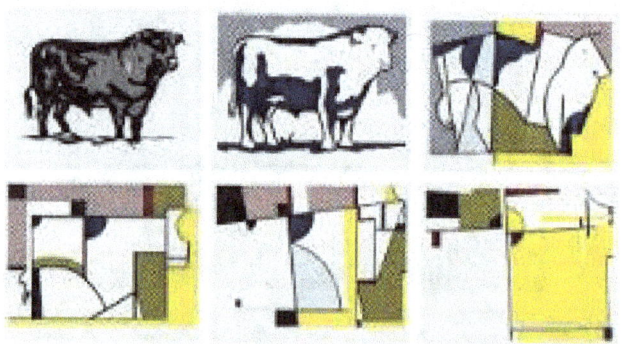

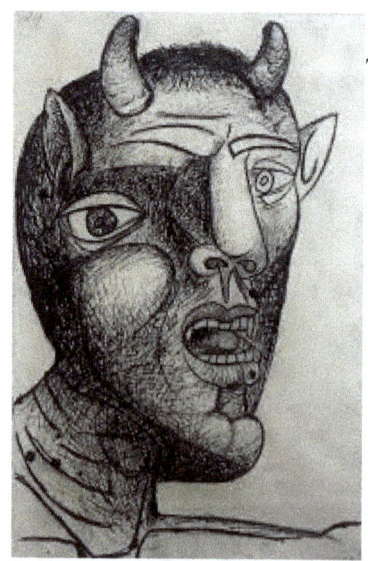

Pablo Picasso

The Minotaur

Futurism

From Futurism They both despised the war ideal , but they saved the research for movement in art . Umberto Boccioni , Fortunato De Pero and Giacomo Balla were the most influencing . They were well influential also on the theatre scenographies , so all of them who worked for the theatre including Chagall Marc and Duchamp came to know them .

The gun was included both by Surrealism and by Pop Art .

Balla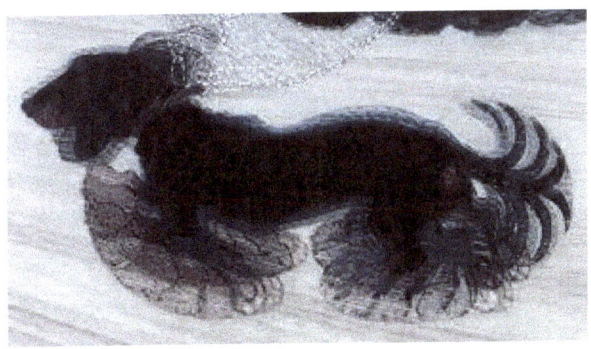

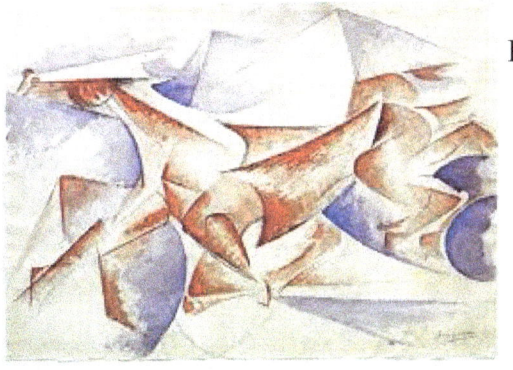 Boccioni

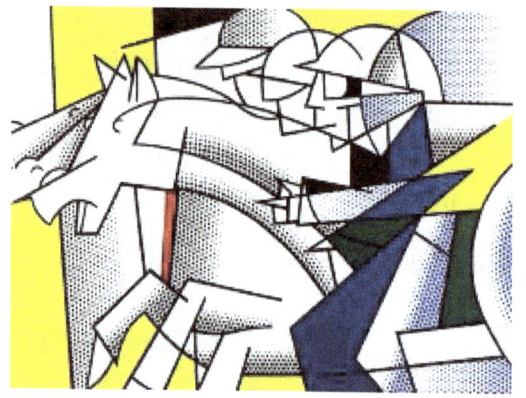

Roy Lichtenstein

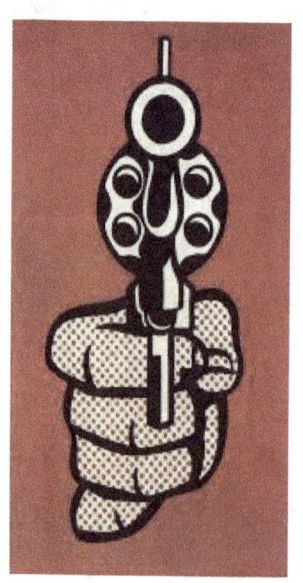

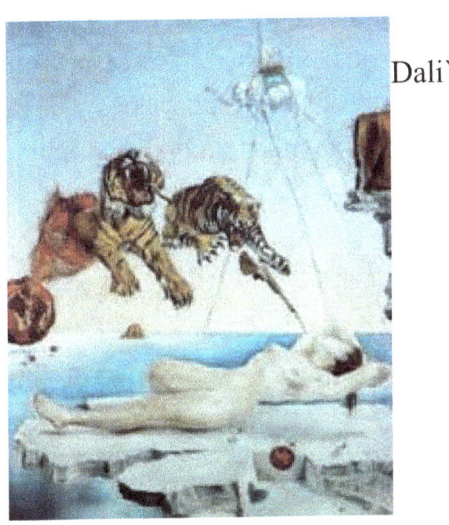 Dali`

The explosion of the atomic bomb made the atomic time
explode by itself

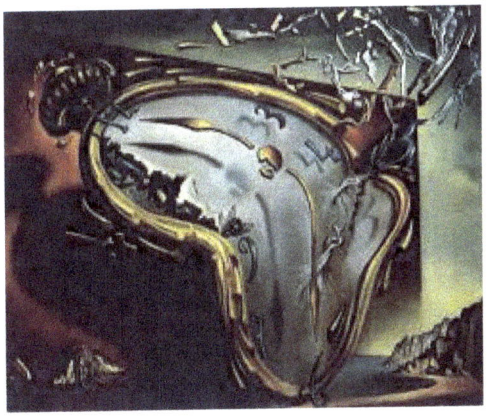

Abstractism

From abstractism they derived the use of primary colours , the black line such as the one used in cartoons or in photography , and the geometric and biomorph shapes of Vassily Kandisky , Piet Mondrian and the metal modular sculpture by Lazslo Moholy Nagy .

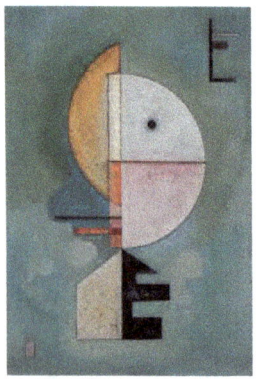 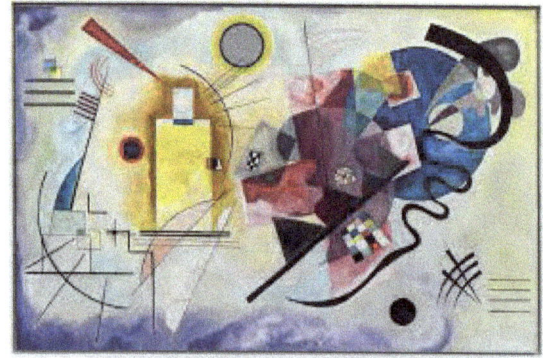

Vassily Kandinsky

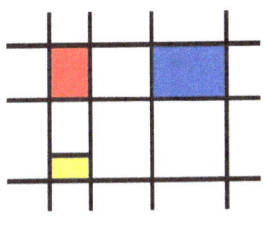 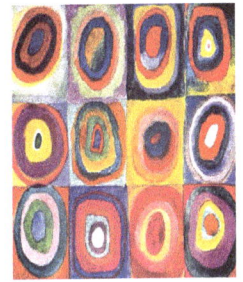 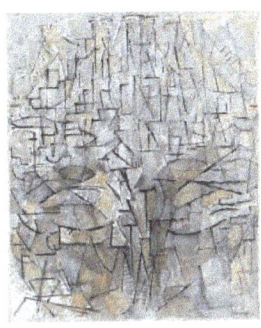

Piet Mondrian

Laszlo Moholy Nagy

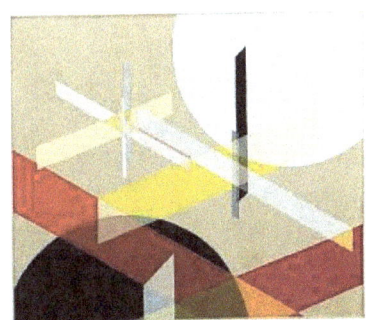 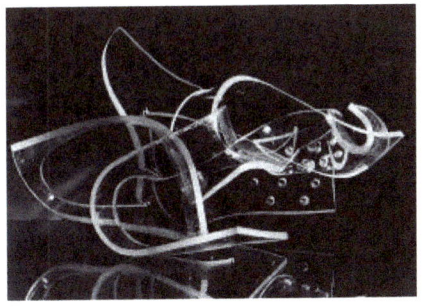

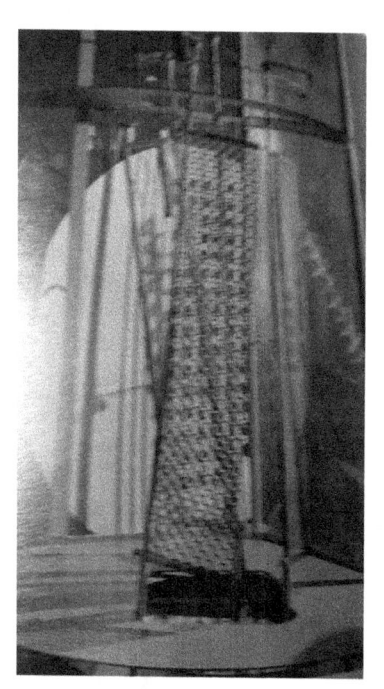

Metaphysical

In philosophy Metaphysics studies the prime precepts that are not perceived by sensory experiences . It is translated into parallel realities and enigmatic spaces , Giorgio de Chirico is the master painter of reference . He introduced nonsense of life , enigmas , rebus , eerie objects , and neoclassical elements .His symbols are antropomorphic horses , Ferrara his city of birth and himself masked and previous masterpieces.

From him they derived the myth of the self ego .

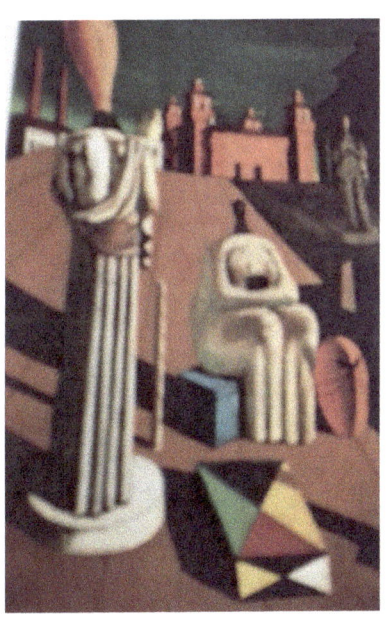 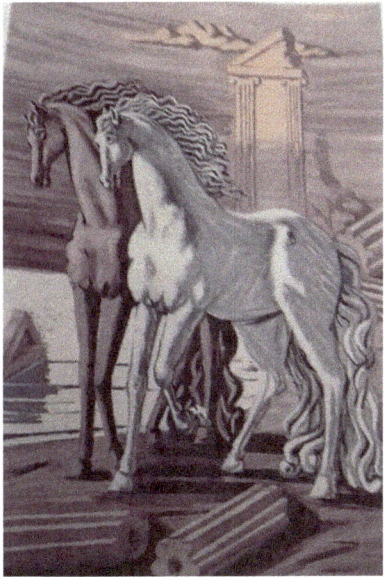

Roy Lichtenstein

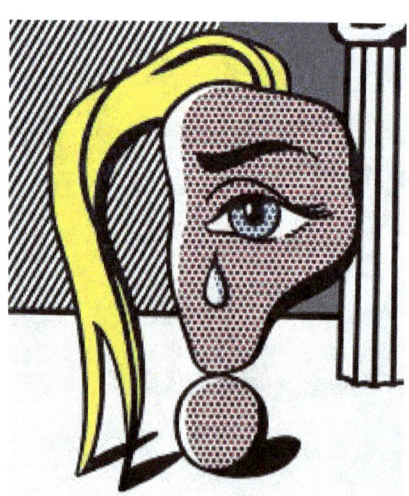

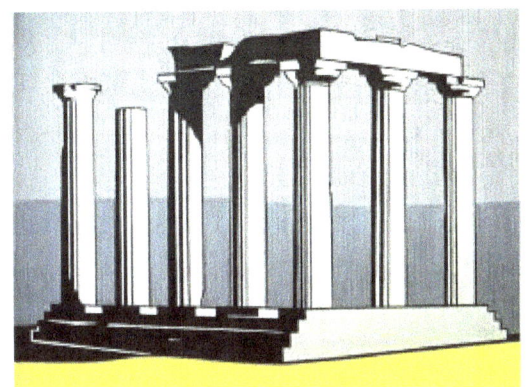

2. Dada

Further to what we have already seen there is in the movement a research of the mixture of different materials to leave the image or the impression or to express the emotions of the author . Author who is undecided if to remain anonymous or to play with its name in a nonsense full of sense . The collage should give eternity through the future. They are projected towards a fluxus of images. Past and present tend to the future.

What`s the meaning of Dada ? The word is everything and nothing . In Russian is a double assertion , In German a double "There" in Italian it is the blubbering of a child . Jean Arp wrote that the word was invented by Tristran Tzara at the Cafe` de la Terrasse in Zurich in 1916 , the birth year of the movement. For some Africans is the sacred cow tail , in French is a rocking horse and in Roumanian it means "Ok you`re right Don`t talk about it anymore".

In fact it started at the Cabaret Voltaire in Zurich where international refugees like James Joyce or Lenin where playing chess with Marcel Duchamp , Dali` Salvador or Hugo Ball , Tristran Tzara or Max Ernst. They gave value in an antiwar atmosphere to irrationality and nonsense , rejecting the correlation between words and meaning , capitalism and consumerism vs communism , debauchery and existentialism.

The audience merged with the performers in a sort of liberation spirit , the fragments of humankind were restored in use of nonsense , jokes (betises) and nudism .

Then it spread to Berlin in 1917 , in New York in 1918 and in Paris in the early twenties . The roaring twenties . The dadaist gatherings included demonstrations , performances , publications of art or literature , sound poetry , sculpture , cut up , ready made objects , and collage, further to photo montage.

It influenced downtown music , jazz , surrealism , new dada and pop art and fluxus which major exponent is Yoko Ono.

Dada portfolio: Marcel Duchamp Copy Seduction Venice

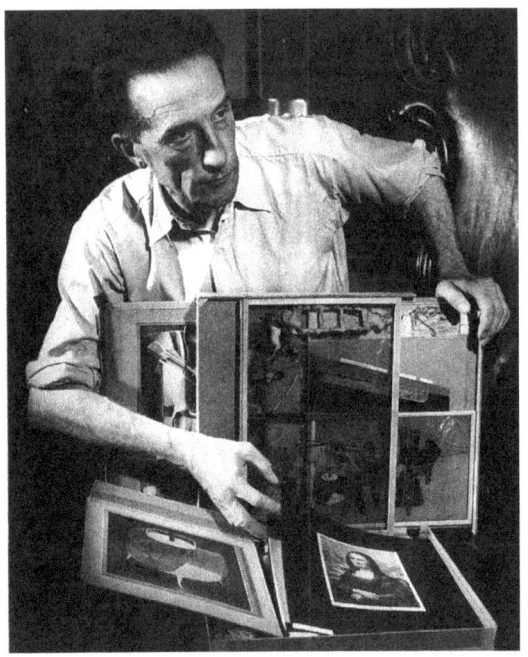

Hans Jean Arp

He was a German French sculptor and painter and poet
(1886/1966)

In 1916 he belonged to Dadaism in Zurich , while in 1920 he
opened it in Cologne together with Max Ernst and Alfred
Grunwald .

In 1926 he was in Paris and switched under the influence of
Henry Bergson to Surrealism while in the 30s he switched
materials , started sculpture with stone and bronze in Abstract
art .

In the 50s he went to New York where he opened his gallery.

He returned to Switzerland , Basel in 1966 where he died.

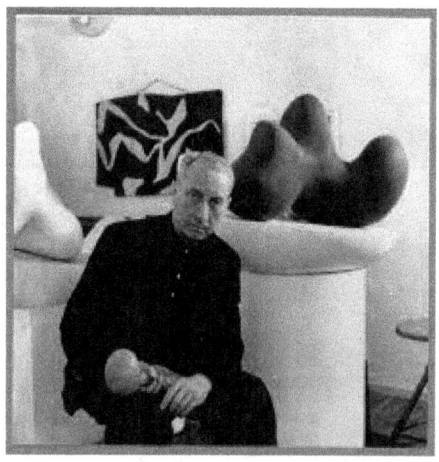

Hans Arp works

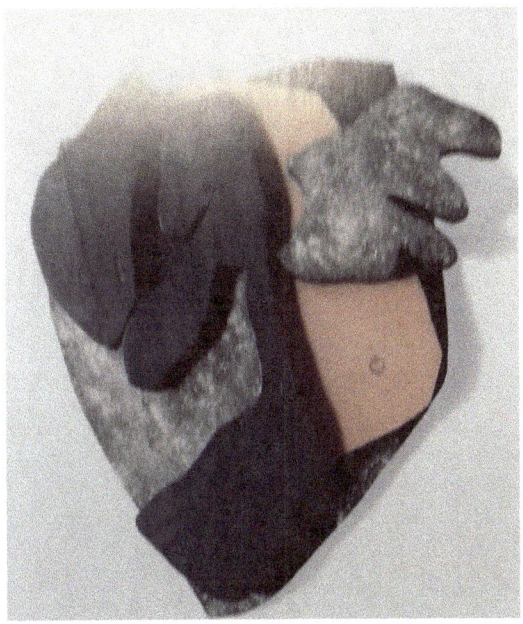

This is a summarizing work of Jean Arp called the bird going to meet the butterfly. You can see the bird on the right and the butterfly with open wings , a sort of moth for the dark colours on the the left . The sky is pink and the background silver .

It could be love between man and woman in a pink heart , or the flight of life towards death in the good and bad days of humankind .The material is wood.

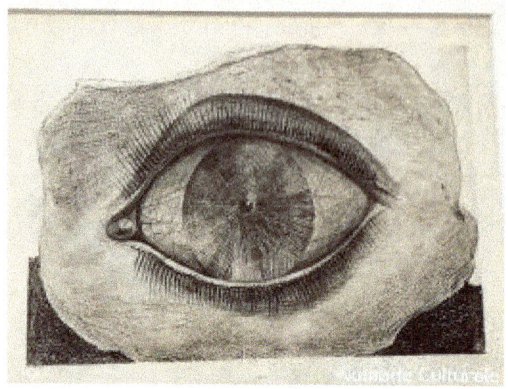

The eye in stone and papier mache is already Surrealist you
will see the difference in expression with Rene` Magritte.

Max Ernst

German Painter sculptor print maker graphic artist and poet he was naturalised American and French .(1891/1976).

Influenced by Cubism and Van Gogh , he invented grattage and frottage .

In 1914 he met his long life friend Hans Jean Arp in Cologne .

In 1919 he met Paul Klee and studied in Munich with Giorgio de Chirico.

In the 1920s in Paris he met Gala Eluard and Breton . He collaborated with Joan Miro` for a ballet for Diaghelev.

In 1941 he arrived in New York with Peggy Guggenheim , Marcel Duchamp and Marc Chagall.

In 1946 his marriage to Guggenheim did not last and he had a double marriage with his friend Man Ray , he to Dorothea Tanning and Man Ray with Browner.From the 1950s he lived mainly in France where he died in Paris.

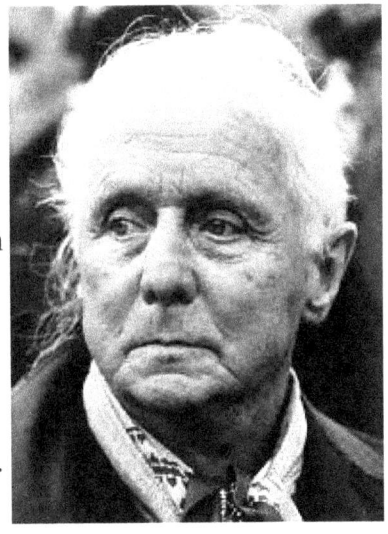

Max Ernst works

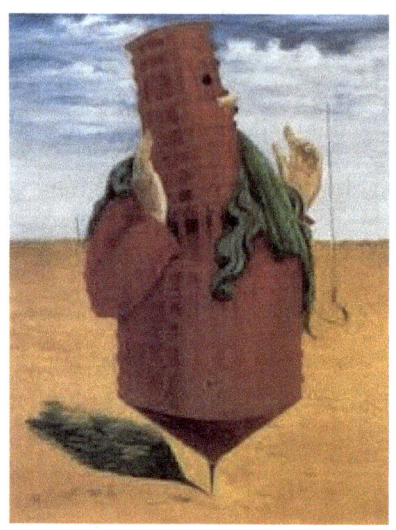

Ubu Imperator is a surrealist /dadaist work were the bird which he called ubu or lolop is dresses as a fashionable dandy of the times , reminding Picabia and his scarves , and wearing white gloves , but his stability is precarious being only a sting on the soil . The desert around him is the wasteland of society where the author lived , A harsh criticism about some people attitudes and society , the sky is after storm and the ubu seems to call for help.

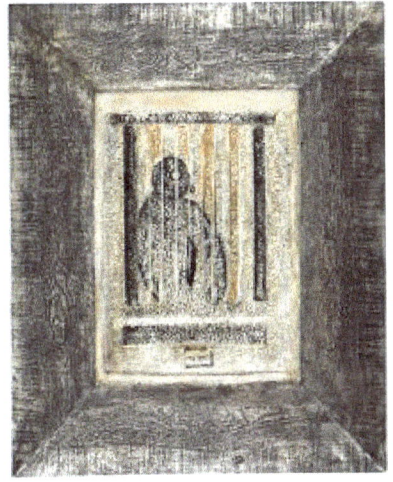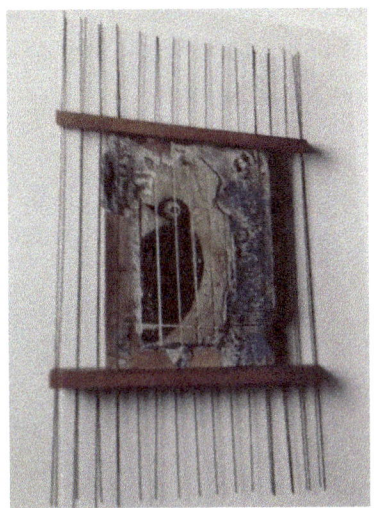

The bird is not in cage is the title of these two series of lolop .

In fact there is ambivalence between the palisade of the window and the cage of the bird . Is the artist free to compose or he has to follow the rules of society ? This is the question it seems to suggest.

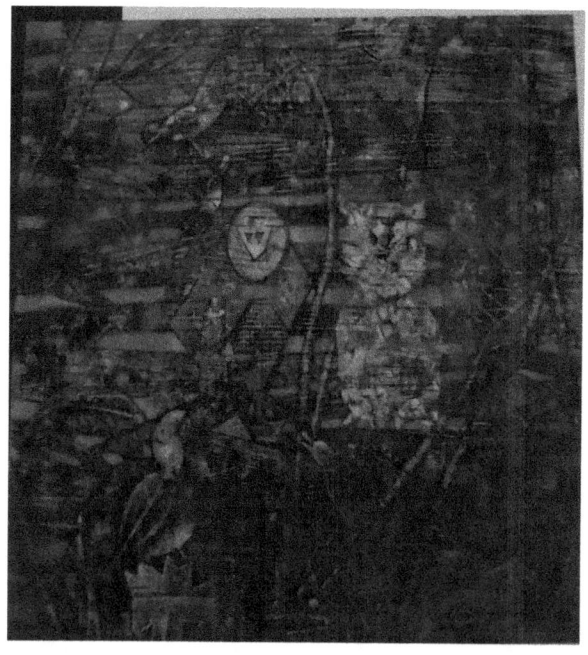

Here we are in a forest where birds of different species can be detached from the owl on the right to the parrot at the bottom left . His influence are the fauves and it is a typical description of the different souls of artistry that reigned in the surrealist group movement .

Marcel Duchamp

French painter sculptor chess player writer associated with Dada Cubism and conceptual art . (1887/1968)

Long lasting friend of Francis Picabia he met during World War I , they went together travelling in 1912 and in 1917 they adhered to Dada.

He invented the ready made objects .

He stayed in New York and in the 1920s with the help of Man Ray he created the Kinetik works.

His dada unconventional works of art are expressed also by ancient reproductions innovated like the moustachioed Mona Lisa.

Sometimes he dressed as a woman Rrose Selavy alias Arroser la vie , wet the life or enjoy life, as such he invented the perfume of life , the bottle of which cost an enormous amount.

On returning to Europe in the 1930s he switched to chess and became a professional chess player . Samuel Beckett , his friend , wrote "Endgame" in 1957 telling about his obsession of the White-Black final draw.

He lived mainly at Greenwich Village New York but went to die in France.

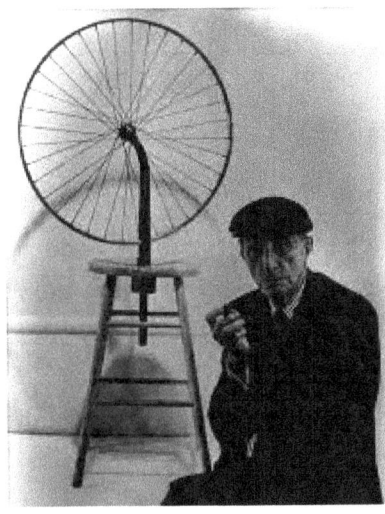

This is the portrait of Marcel Duchamp with his first ready made object , a stool surmounted by a bicycle wheel.

The ready made was an object already existing de contextualised and rebuilt to schock or express something different from its previous use . In this object the two become a form of art for art`s sake.

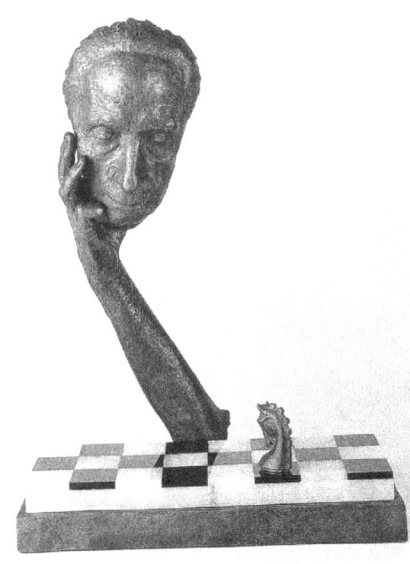

Marcel Duchamp left the Surrealist because they quarelled too much and became a professional chess player , here in Portrait of the board we can see his durable cult of self plu his endgame which inspired the theatre of Beckett.

Man Ray

American visual painter , fashion and portrait photographer (1890/1976) alias of Emmauel Radnitzky.

In the 1920s in New York he adhered to Dada, friend of Tzara.

In Paris in 1923 he created rayographs , photos with cameraless photograms and solarization with Lee Miller his colleague and model. He used ready made objects and affection objects.

In 1946 he married Browner who was a dancer with Martha Graham in Hollywood.

He returned to Paris in the 1950s where he died in 1976 for a lung infection.

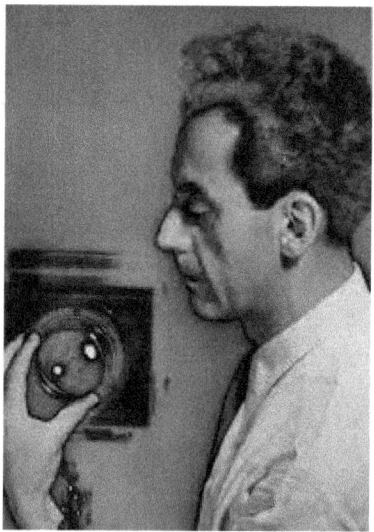

Man Ray `s works

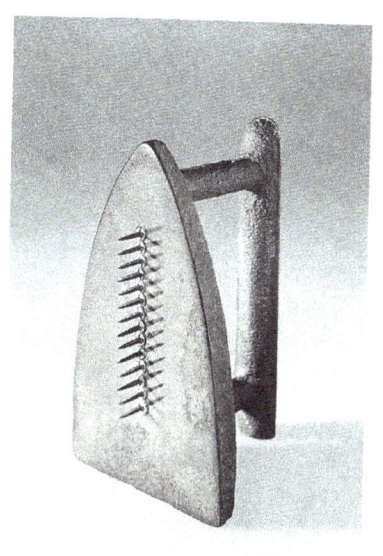

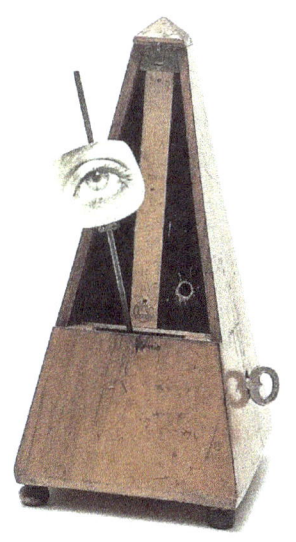

↑ 20.314 **Man Ray**, *Cadeau*, 1964 (copia di un originale perduto del 1921). *Ready-made* rettificato: ferro da stiro con 14 chiodi saldati sulla piastra, altezza 16,3 cm. Gerusalemme, Israel Museum.

↑ 20.315 **Man Ray**, *Oggetto indistruttibile (o Oggetto da distruggere)*, 1964 (copia dell'originale del 1923), 22,5×11×11,6 cm. New York, Museum of Modern Art.

The ready made were the dadaist objects he created , the first is an iron with nails and it is called Present . There are different legends about the making of the object .

The second is a metronome with the eye of Lee Miller his model and girlfriend of the time . It was made in a serie , at first the eye meant the love of being watched , then the object that he longed for but that he had lost , and next the object to be forgiven and forgotten .

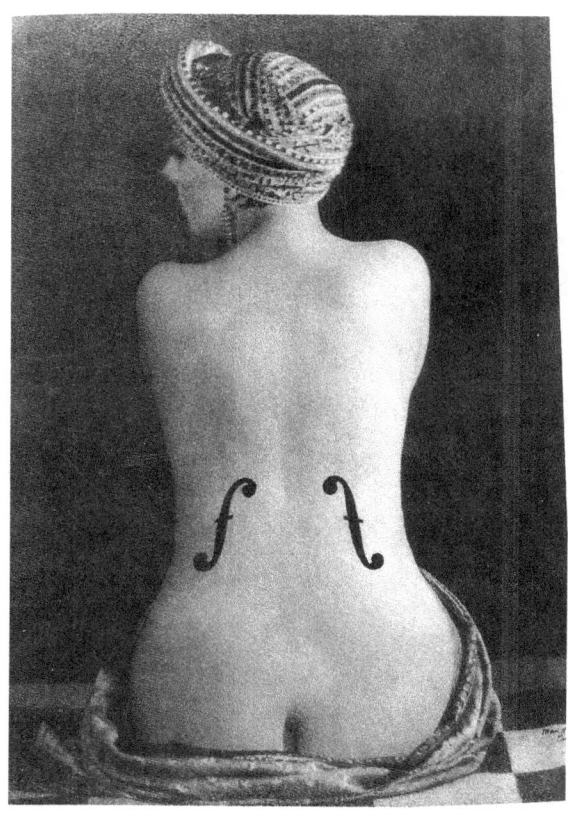

Kiki of Montparnasse was the model for this cello , the work is a new concept of ready made using a real person playing the part . The sensuality and the popularity of the work made it become a saying in everyday life , that the proportion of the bottom side of a woman is like a string instrument.

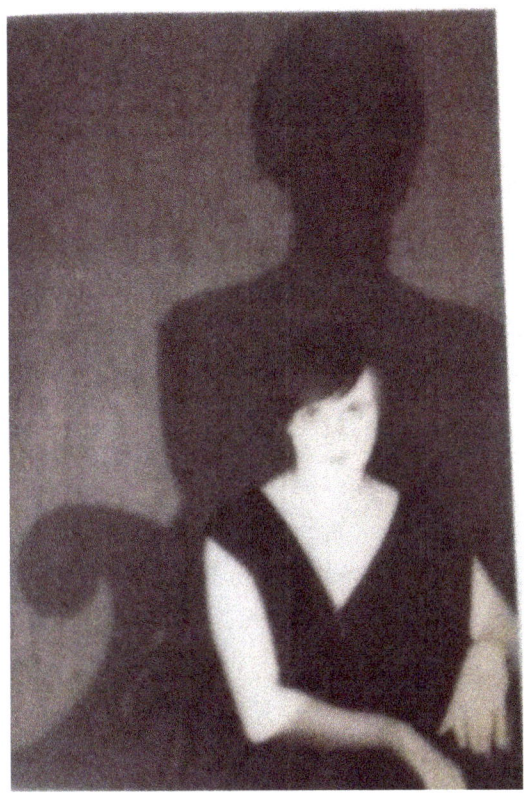

The portrait of Nelly Van Doesburg a talented pianist is of 1923 .She was a lover and model as Lee Miller and Kiki , they met Tristran Tzara and had a long correspondence which influenced also the musical creations of the pianist in Rhytmus.

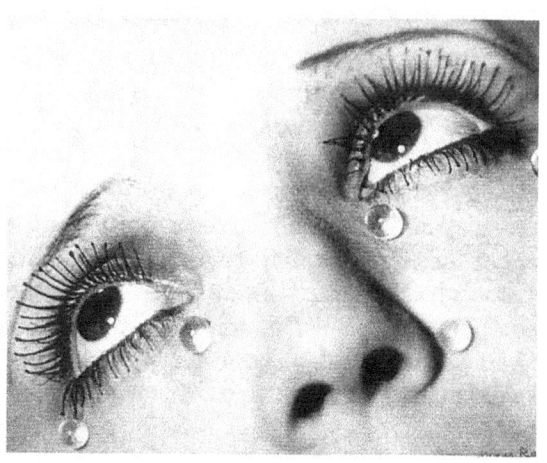

Lee Miller was a photographer colleague and model and girlfriend of Man Ray , here she is portrayed with the application of false glass tears.

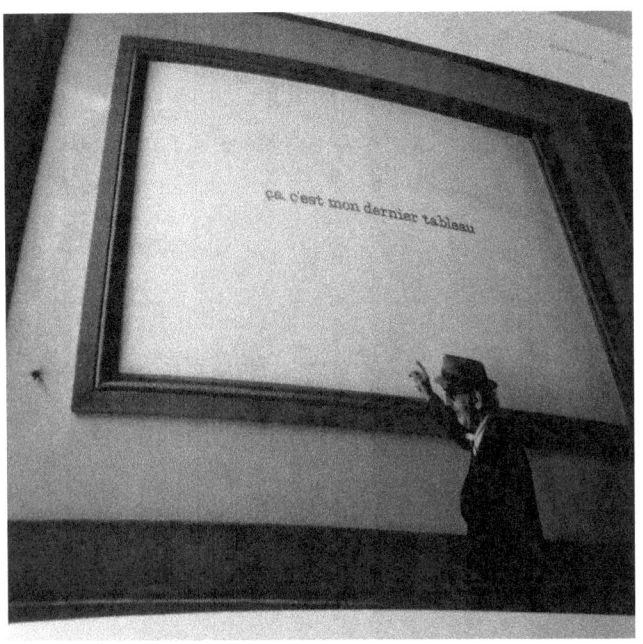

This is my last work of art says the writing in the middle of the white screen framed as if it was a work of art and Man Ray is showing it with a certain demure as if he was not the artist .

Here Man Ray is between Dada and New Dada Pop in the research for the self and the irony to the audience of which he is one .

Luis Picabia

Avant gard painter poet and typographist of Spanish and French origin (1879/1953).

In 1911 he met Marcel Duchamp . He was keen on biology and technology.

In 1915 he was in New York where he met Man Ray and became addict to alcohol and drugs.

He continued his dada adventure in Zurich and Paris till 1924 when he quarrelled with Breton , had a fight and went to trial.

In 1930s he became a close friend of Gertrude Stein , the American novelist and mecenas.

During World War II he was in Algeria and then in 1946 he returned in France where he died in Paris.

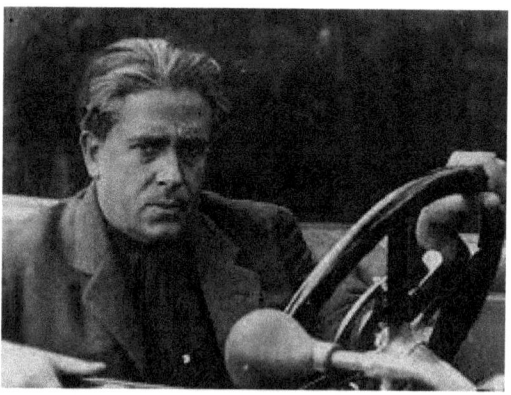

Works of Luis Picabia

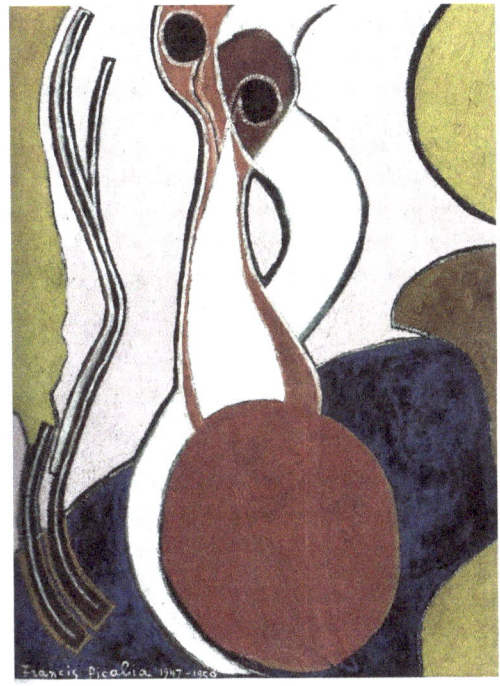

This is one of the summative works of Luis Picabia , the influence is Cubism and Dadaism . We can see two beings beating with the same heart or the time beating into the white fuse . The title is the force of life .

3. Surrealism

Surrealism is an art and cultural movement that developed in Europe in the aftermath of World War I in which artists aimed to allow the unconscious mind to express itself, often resulting in the depiction of illogical or dreamlike scenes and ideas. Its intention was, according to leader André Breton, to "resolve the previously contradictory conditions of dream and reality into an absolute reality, a super-reality", or surreality. It produced works of painting, writing, theatre, film making, photography, and other media as well.

Works of Surrealism feature the element of surprise, unexpected juxtapositions and non sequitur. However, many Surrealist artists and writers regard their work as an expression of the philosophical movement first and foremost (for instance, of the "pure psychic automatism" Breton speaks of in the first Surrealist Manifesto), with the works themselves being secondary, i.e., artifacts of surrealist experimentation.

Leader Breton was explicit in his assertion that Surrealism was, above all, a revolutionary movement.

At the time, the movement was associated with political causes such as communism and anarchism. It was influenced by the Dada movement of the 1910s.

The term "Surrealism" originated with Guillaume Apollinaire in 1917. However, the Surrealist movement was not officially established until after October 1924, with the Surrealist Manifesto published by French poet and critic André Breton. The most important center of the movement was Paris,France. From the 1920s onward, the movement spread around the globe, impacting the visual arts, literature, film, and music of many countries and languages, as well as political thought and practice, philosophy, and social theory.

Freud's work with free association, dream analysis, and the unconscious was of utmost importance to the Surrealists in developing methods to liberate imagination.

In 1925 an autonomous Surrealist group formed in Brussels. The group included the musician, poet, and painter and writer René Magritte, Paul Nougé, Marcel Lecomte, and André Souris.

In 1927 they were joined by the writer Louis Scutenaire. They corresponded regularly with the Paris group, and in 1927 both Goemans and Magritte moved to Paris and frequented Breton's circle. The artists, with their roots in Dada and Cubism, the abstraction of Wassily Kandinsky, Expressionism, and Post-

Impressionism, also reached to older "bloodlines" or proto-surrealists such as Hieronymus Bosch, and the primitive and naive arts.

In the 1920s the influence of Miró and the drawing style of Picasso is visible with the use of fluid curving and intersecting lines and colour, whereas the first takes a directness that would later be influential in movements such as Pop art.

Giorgio de Chirico, and his previous development of metaphysical art, was one of the important joining figures between the philosophical and visual aspects of Surrealism.

His images,including set designs for the Ballets Russes, would create a decorative form of Surrealism, and he would be an influence on the two artists who would be even more closely associated with Surrealism in the public mind: Dalí and Magritte. He would, however, leave the Surrealist group in 1928.

In 1924, Miró and Masson applied Surrealism to painting. The first Surrealist exhibition, La Peinture Surrealiste, was held at Galerie Pierre in Paris in 1925. It displayed works by Masson, Man Ray, Paul Klee,Miró, and others. The show confirmed that Surrealism had a component in the visual arts (though it had been initially debated whether this was possible), and techniques from Dada, such as photomontage, were used. The following year, on March 26, 1926, Galerie Surréaliste opened with an exhibition by Man Ray.

Breton published Surrealism and Painting in 1928 which summarized the movement to that point, though he continued to update the work until the 1960s.

Famous Surrealist photographers are the American Man Ray, the French/Hungarian Brassaï, French Claude Cahun and the Dutch Emiel van Moerkerken.

As a movement it influenced also music like jazz or contemporary classic with Poulenc and Varese.

Dalí and Magritte created the most widely recognized images of the movement. Dalí joined the group in 1929 and participated in the rapid establishment of the visual style between 1930 and 1935.

Surrealism as a visual movement had found a method: to expose psychological truth; stripping ordinary objects of their normal significance, to create a compelling image that was beyond ordinary formal organization, in order to evoke empathy from the viewer.

Long after personal, political and professional tensions fragmented the Surrealist group, Magritte and Dalí continued to define a visual program in the arts. This program reached beyond painting, to encompass photography as well, as can be seen from a Man Ray self-portrait, whose use of assemblage influenced Robert Rauschenberg's collage boxes.

During the 1930s Peggy Guggenheim, an important American art collector, married Max Ernst and began promoting work by other Surrealists such as Yves Tanguy and the British artist John Tunnard.

The early work of many Pop Artists reveals a tight bond between the more superficial aspects of both movements, the aspects of Dadaistic humor in such artists as Rauschenberg and the cultural criticism of surrealism .

Frida Kahlo should be mentioned. She had a New York solo exhibition in 1938 with 25 paintings, encouraged by Breton himself.

Breton continued to write and espouse the importance of liberating the human mind, as with the publication "The Tower of Light" in 1952.

Breton's return to France after the War, began a new phase of Surrealist activity in Paris, and his critiques of rationalism and dualism found a new audience. Breton insisted that Surrealism was an ongoing revolt against the reduction of humanity to market relationships, religious gestures and misery and to espouse the importance of liberating the human mind.

The events of May 1968 in France included a number of Surrealist ideas, and among the slogans the students spray-painted on the walls of the Sorbonne were familiar Surrealist ones. Joan Miró would commemorate this in a painting titled May 1968.

There were also groups who associated with both currents and were more attached to Surrealism, such as the Revolutionary Surrealist Group.

Many writers from and associated with the Beat Generation were influenced greatly by Surrealists. Philip Lamantia and Ted Joans are often categorized as both Beat and Surrealist writers. Many other Beat writers show significant evidence of Surrealist influence. A few examples include Bob Kaufman, Gregory Corso, Allen Ginsberg,and Lawrence Ferlinghetti. Artaud in particular was very influential to many of the Beats, but especially Ginsberg and Carl Solomon. Ginsberg cites Artaud's "Van Gogh – The Man Suicided by Society" as a direct influence on "Howl", along with Apollinaire's "Zone", García Lorca's "Ode to Walt Whitman", and Schwitters' "Priimiititiii". The structure of Breton's "Free Union" had a significant influence on Ginsberg's "Kaddish". In Paris, Ginsberg and Corso met their heroes Tristan Tzara, Marcel Duchamp, Man Ray, and Benjamin Péret, and to show their admiration Ginsberg kissed Duchamp's feet and Corso cut off Duchamp's tie.

William S. Burroughs, a core member of the Beat Generation and a postmodern novelist, developed the cutup technique with former surrealist Brion Gysin—in which chance is used to dictate the composition of a text from words cut out of other sources—referring to it as the "Surrealist Lark" and recognizing its debt to the techniques of Tristan Tzara.

Salvador Dali`

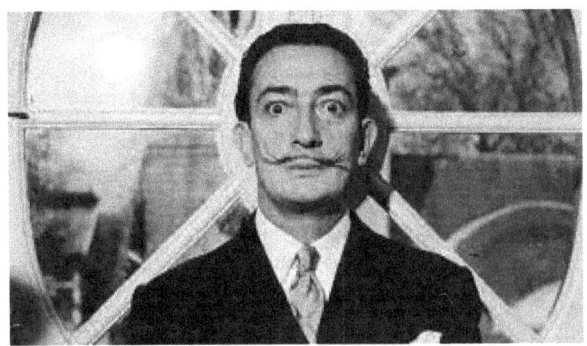

Salvador Dali` I Domenech marquis of Pubol (1904/89)

was a Spanish painter , sculptor , writer , photographer,
filmmaker, designer , scriptwriter and mystic.

He belongs to the two movements of Dada and Surrealism .

In 1924 in Madrid he met Federico Garcia Lorca , his friend ,
and Luis Bunuel.

In 1926 in Paris he met Joan Miro` and Pablo Picasso.

In 1929 he met his long life muse and wife (34 and 58) Gala
Eluard, became a surrealist and was disinherited by his father.

In the 30s and 40s he was in New York keen more on giving
scandals than his works.

In 1951 he returned in Figueres where he built his museum
(1960-74). He had a great influence on Pop art and Warhol.

In 1965 he met his other muse Amanda Lear .

In 1968 he designed the lollipop Chupa Chups .

In 1982 Gala died after long illnesses, and he followed in 1989.

Dali` works

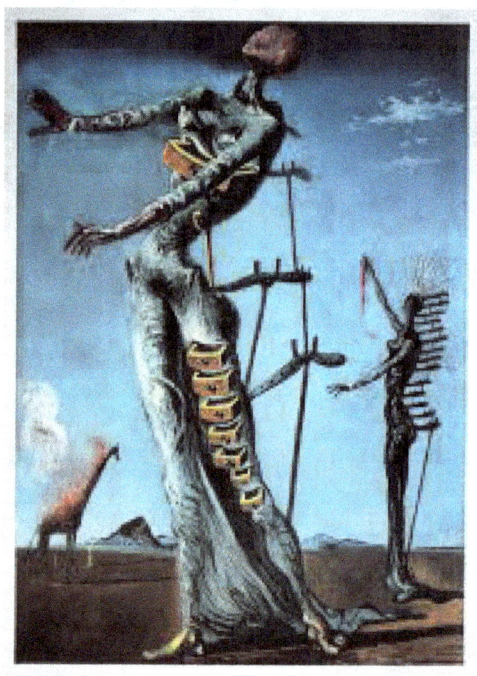

The

drawers woman is a symbol in Dali` of the imperscrutability of
the depth of women . Each drawer has a secret part of life , in a
landscape that is familiar and exotic at the same time , although
life seems at the verge of the end and we could think to be
walking in blindness a white cloud and the blue sky at the
horizon can save us from ourselves .

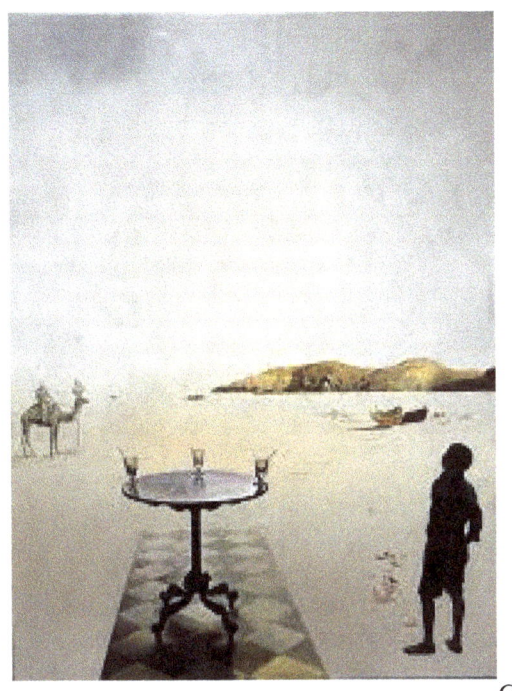

Childhood

by Dali` opens in a desert where there is the dead brother in silhouette , the bourgeois family life in the first front and and exotic camel on the left , his dream of desert , his mirage . What saves him and brigs him to adulthood is the rocky silhouette of woman on the horizon on the right and the familiar port of fishermen near house.

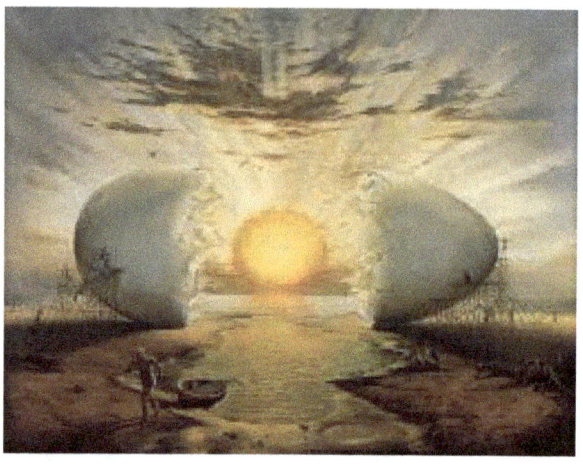

The egg is another of the symbols dear to Dali` .It reminds us of an ambivalent wonderful dawn on man in the port and his ship or the dawn of a new era after the atomic bomb.

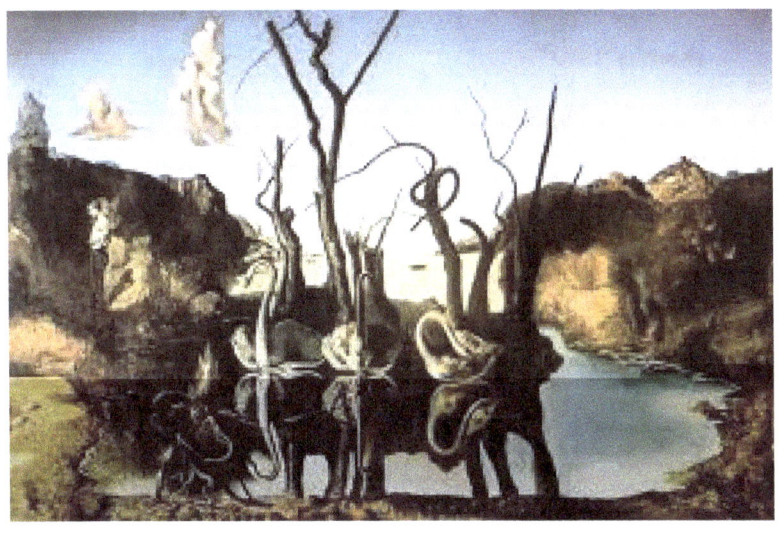

Swans becoming elephants is an original painting showing how
Dali` was good at painting and original in the mirroring of
common European life into the exotic .It is one of his
numberless jokes demonstrating his art. Oniric and dreamlike it
is influenced by the Freudian theory of interpretation of
dreams.

Joan Miro`

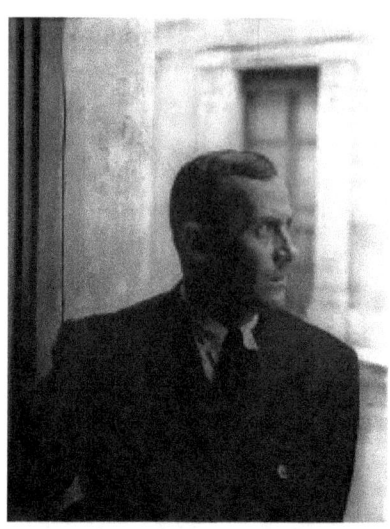

Spanish painter , tile maker and sculptor (1893-1983)

He spent his childhood in Mallorca .

In 1916 he was influenced by fauves.

In 1920 in Paris he met Pablo Picasso , Dali` and Tristran Tzara , collaborated with Max Ernst , Hans Arp and Pierre Bonnard.

In 1929 he married and had a daughter.

During the 30s and 40s he was in Paris then he returned to Mallorca.

In the 50s he obtained success in USA.

In 1972 he built his museum in Barcelona .

From 1978 he devoted himself to the theatre. To be recognized in Spain he had to wait the 1980s . He died in Mallorca in 1983 but his tomb is in Barcelona Montjuic Cemetery.

Miro` s works

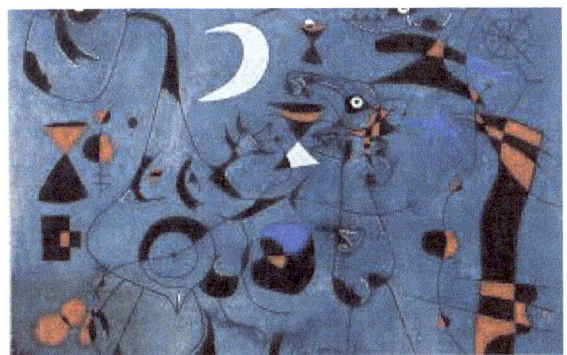

Miro`s painting with influences of biomorph abstractism and the primary colours is full of imagination in a night dream .

The black lines give movement and you can distinguish a woman on the left and a man on the right . Probably a phone call for a romantic date and the couple dancing or rather whirling in the middle .

It is a narrative painting with the modern twist.

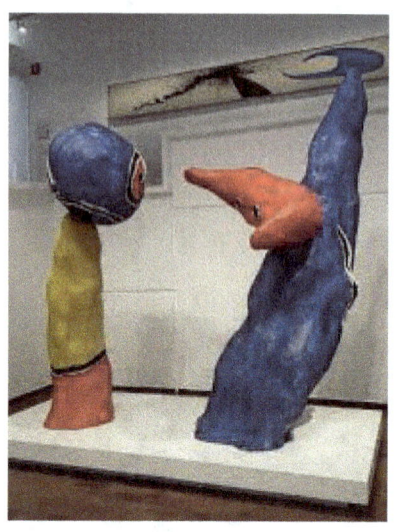

The corrida revisited in this sculpture by Miro` with the bull on the right and the toreador on the left . As you can see nature is winning , primary colours are used , and the ambivalence of sensual interpretation is open with a man on the right and a woman on the left . Sometimes nature is woman , like nature is also the meaning of the corrida , the rush to defy natural death of the toreador who is alone in front of the forces of nature . The aggressive red colour reveals the violence and the submissive head of the man the wheel of fortune we have to subdue under.

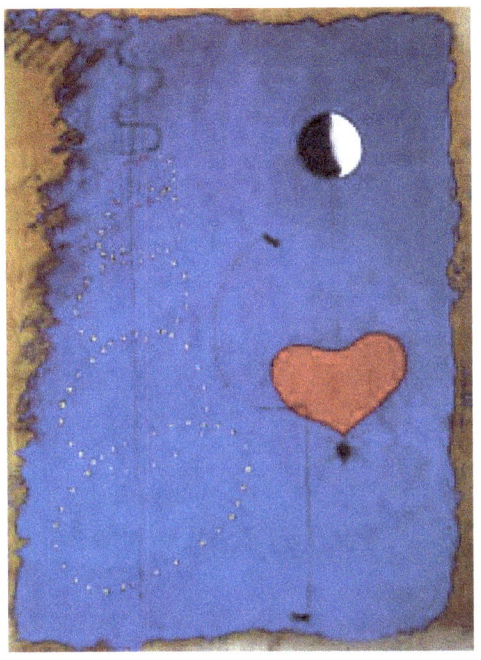

The ballet dancer is another famous painting by Miro` where there is research for movement through lines and points and the surrealistic interpretation of the dancer all passion and heart and with a black and white head , meaning perhaps that although the artist is passionate there are black and white facets of the person.

Rene` Magritte

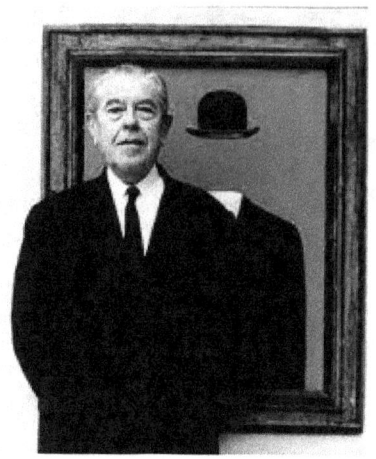

Belgian painter (1898-1967)

He was influenced by Cubism , Futurism and Metaphysical.

In 1922 he marries and becomes a graphic designer.

In 1925 he become s a surrealist in Bruxelles

In 1927 in Paris he met Breton

In the 40s he was at Carcassonne

He died in Bruxelles from pancreas cancer after a long journey between France and Italy.

Magritte`s works

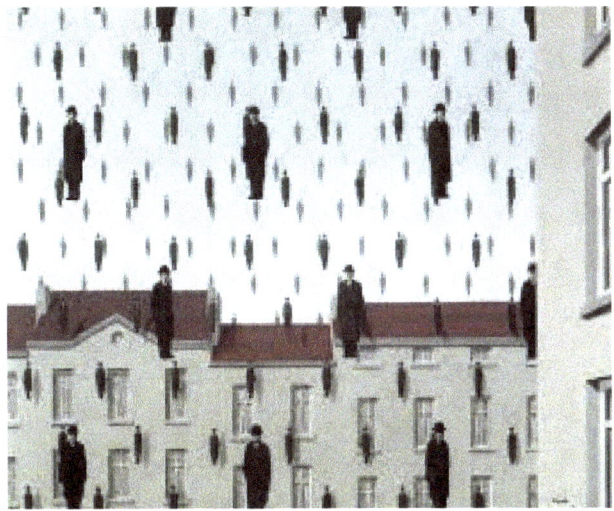

It`s raining men told us a song of Ginger Spice but in Magritte it is surrealistically true.

The symbology is homologation of the society both in the architecture of the houses and the men living into them .

On one side is giving us a gloomy experience and feeling of never have the possibility of freedom and originality on the other is assuming the responsibility of being one of them .

Does the observer think to belong ? The artist in my opinion doesn`t .

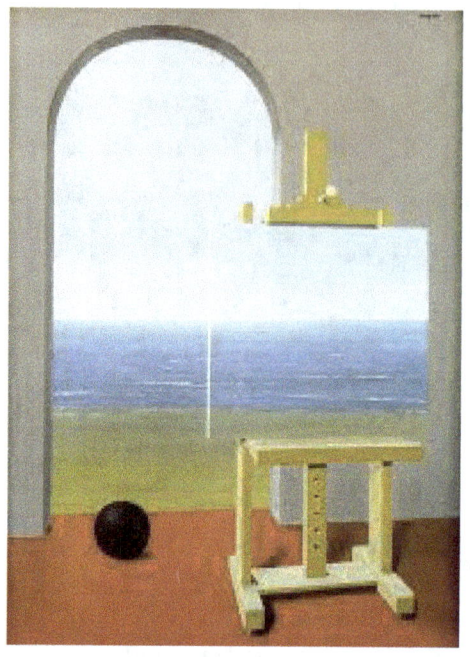

In Magritte we have the juxtaposition between reality and art , the outdoor and indoor and then a surrealistic portrait of the painter with his head like a sphere upside down .

The open door is open to interpretation , it is the observer who must actively comment upon.

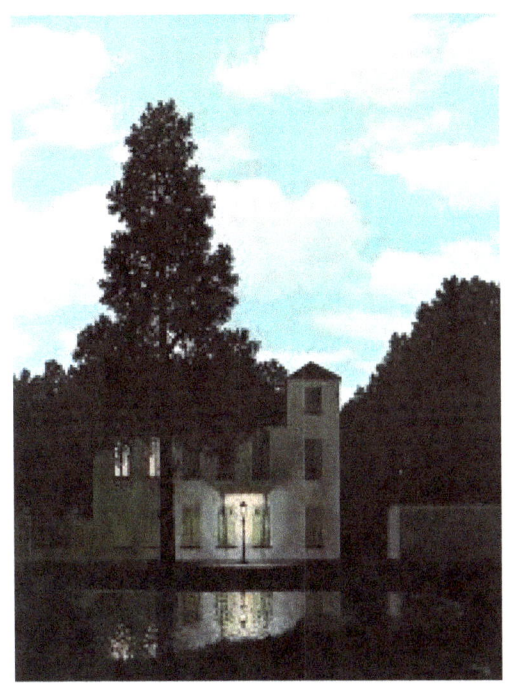

Reflections by day and night is a masterpiece of the Guggenheim in Venice . The two reflections in water and sky differ during that time of the day when evening has begun but day has not left the day yet . The lights in the street and in the house are masked by shadows and the tree silhouette .

The intriguing mix makes us ask who inhabits the house.

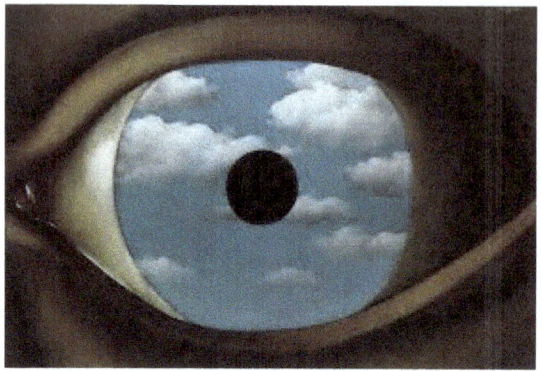

The eye was a symbol of dada and the surrealists , a saying
says one can see the soul of man in his eye , therefore the eye is
blue and the sky full of sunny clouds.

Impressive and happy at the same time , it is interesting that it
is the left eye since the Surrealists declare themselves leftists
and anarchists.

Yves Tanguy

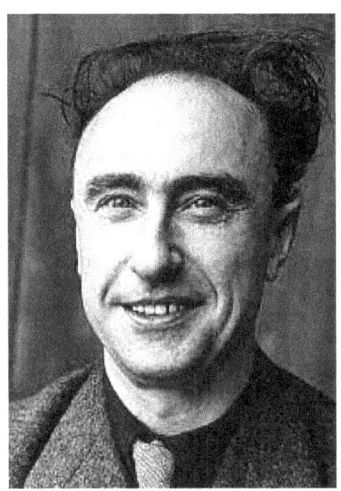

French painter naturalised American (1900-1955)

In Paris he met Henri Matisse.

During 1918 as a soldier he met his friend Jacques Prevert

He was influenced by Giorgio de Chirico.

In 1924 he went to live in Paris with Prevert and met Breton.

In 1940 he married paintress Kay Ange and lived in Connecticut

In 1955 he died of a cerebral haemorrage.

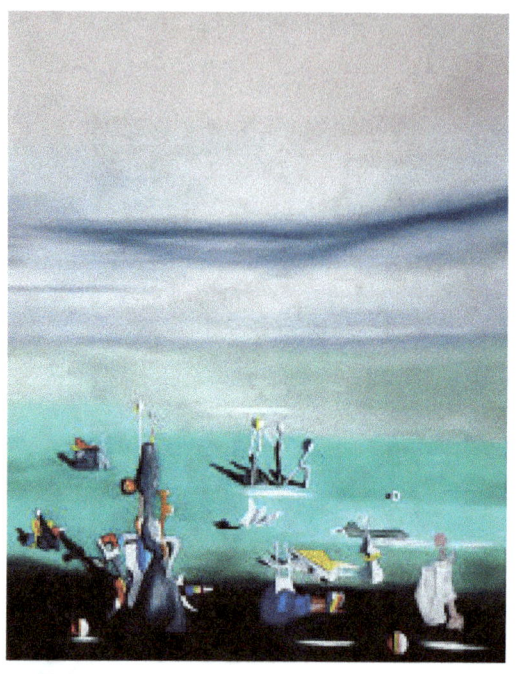

The paiting is called Time and again . It is a reflection upon childhood and family in a serene landscape . Though time in black is invading the life of mankind like an petroleum staining the happiness of childhood and years past .

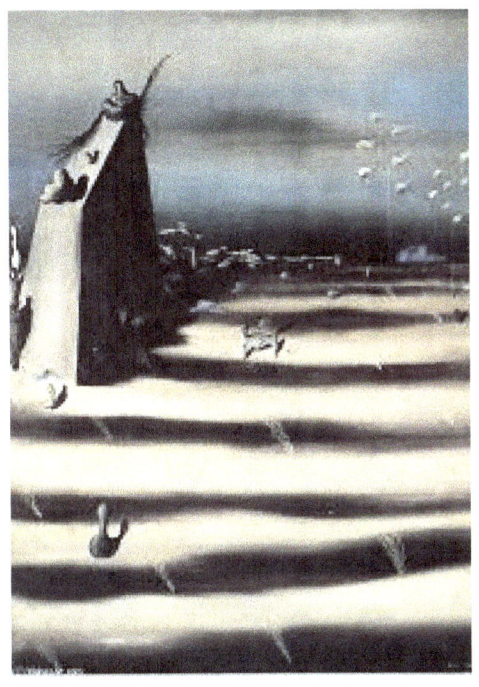

The desert of memory is a compart of dunes or a roof of a house with chimney from which we can see trees or clouds upon tree . It is influenced by Metaphysical and Symbolism.

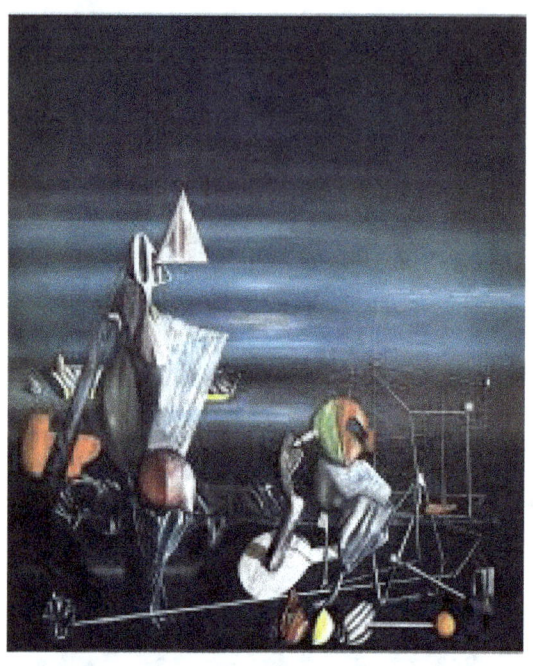

My generation is full of music , jazzy probably , a web of metal
and a man like an artifact of triangles or pyramids and spheres.

The background is gloomy and nightmarish but the ensemble
seems ready to start the concert of life.

Maurits Escher

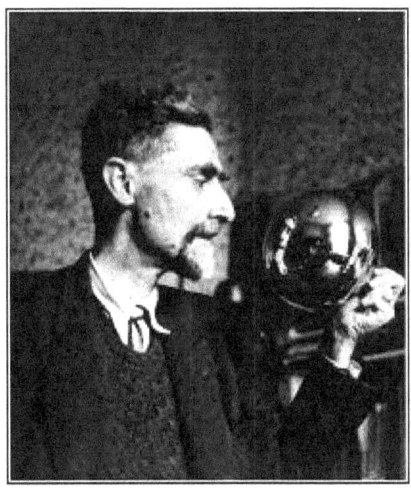

Dutch engraver and designer (1898-1972)

In 1922 he visited Italy where he started to live

In 1923 he met Julia Umiker whom he married the following year

In 1935 He moved with family to Switzerland Zurich

In 1937 he was in Belgium and then back in the Netherlands

In 1964 he had a surgery in Canada , his wife left him and he returned to the Netherlands

In 1969 he designer an LP cover for the Rolling Stones

He died in 1972.

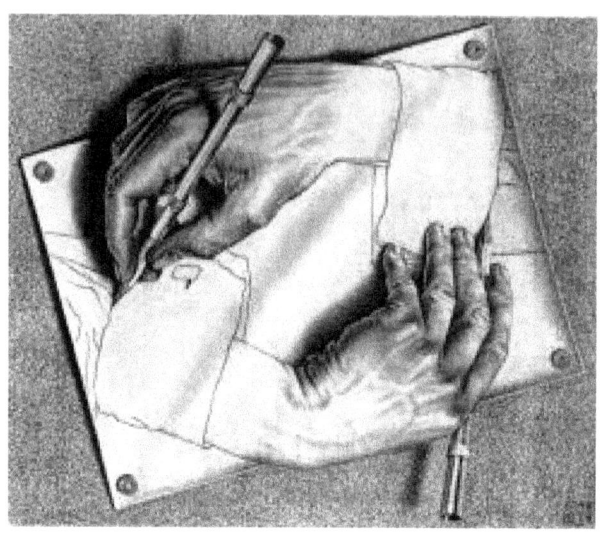

Her Escher is showing hands that are creating themselves , the author who had an awful college experiences in fact is self made artist , coming out of his experience of graphic designer and learning from the Italian ancient painters how through sufferance and practice you can obtain success and wealth.

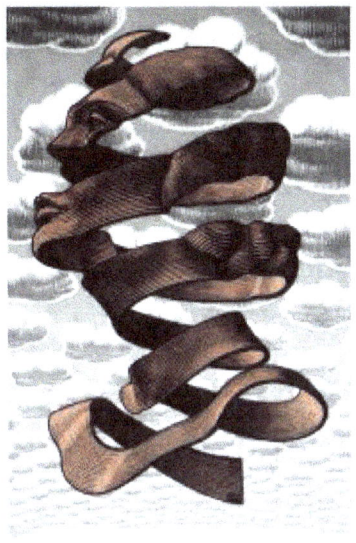

In this self portrait through and apple peel or ribbon we have
the essence of Surrealism . Notice the clouds in the background
the idea of apple peel as poison of woman or ribbon as female
attribute and the making of the man through imagination and
the female support .Two clouds are stormy at the top level
while the others are white like sheep , like the audience who is
unable to discern the originality of the author`s creation.

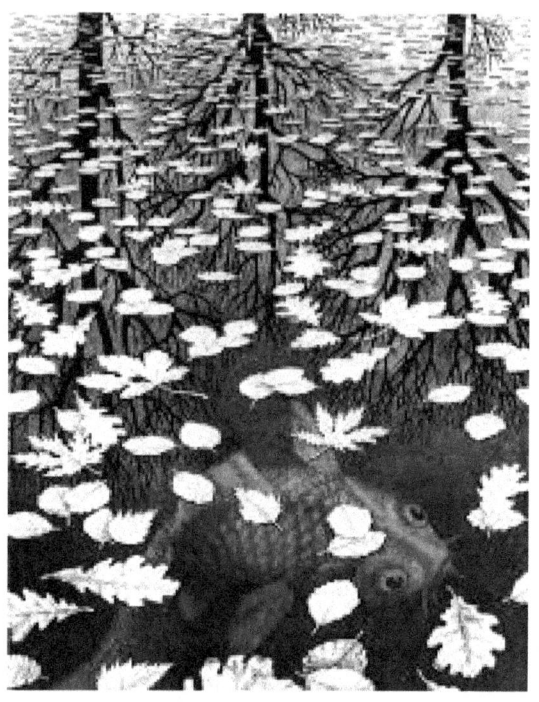

The xerigraphy called three worlds is in fact soil with deep roots and trees , reflected into water where the leaves are floating and carp in the deep of the water . The symbol remind of nipponism with the carp the sacred fish and the autumnal landscape . It exists in different colours all of bronze , brown beige hue variety.

4. New Dada and Pop Art

Pop art or popular art is a movement born in Uk and USA during the second half of the 1950s. The movement represented a challenge to art traditions including images from mass culture and popular media like ads , cartoons and gadgets. One of its aims was to emphasize everyday objects as objects of art mostly through irony. It is associated to copying and rendering techniques , design and photocopying or serial reproduction.

The materials are removed and de-contextualized from the original , isolated or combined with other materials.

In the second post war period new products which gave form to consumerism enter the life of mankind

For example cars, posters, fridges, washing machines , cans , detergents or fizzy drinks. They become the symbols of a consumerist society where pop is born . New Dada and Pop Art have therefore a critical view of society and its growing consumerism.

The city is full of waste and the works of art are therefore serialized and critical. The city becomes a scenery full of contradictions and aggressive or evil, but at the same time lively and familiar to the artist who cannot do without them.

We can define this movement as a modern realism enveloping the changes of its environment .

In the 50s the French philosopher Roland Barthes stated that society give a safe value to the communication through mass media , to the collective conscience which maintains itself serene thanks to the veneration of objects of common use.

Marshall McLuhan said that the evolution of the mass media were fundamental in communication and the artists should confirm it into their art.

There are many different techniques in Pop Art from serial reproduction through stencils , frottage , vynil painting , collage , giant forms , glass sculpture , plastic moulds etc.

On one side they recovered the original techniques of the twentieth century avant garde from dadaism to Cubism but they added also a part of improvisation in the happenings and performances in front of the audience.

The main theme is the existentialist anxiety of the consumerism society where man is detached and annihilated by objects. The interest of the artist is in the images , in everyday life of man and in the artificial world where he lives.

In the works of art the world is coloured , full of life and entertainments while it hides anxiety and sadness. Television radio cinema and commercials enter into the sculpture and the painting as if were impossible to live without them.

The union between the modern reality of mass media and art is popular art.

The pop artists though never comment upon what they represent . The new codes of mass media and the new popular objects are left to the scrutinizing of the audience and to their personal reaction .

The audience becomes an active transformer of the work of art , and Warhol told us that every man would like to have his five minutes notoriety in good or bad .

Andy Warhol

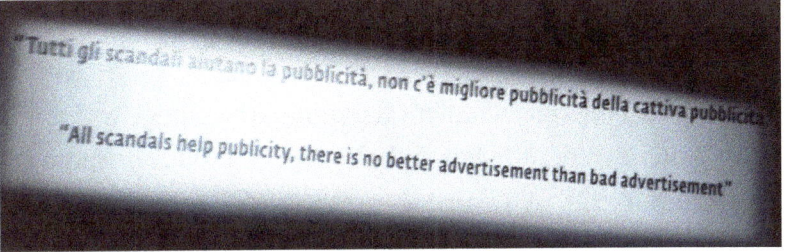

"Tutti gli scandali aiutano la pubblicità, non c'è migliore pubblicità della cattiva pubblicità"

"All scandals help publicity, there is no better advertisement than bad advertisement"

Andy Warhol

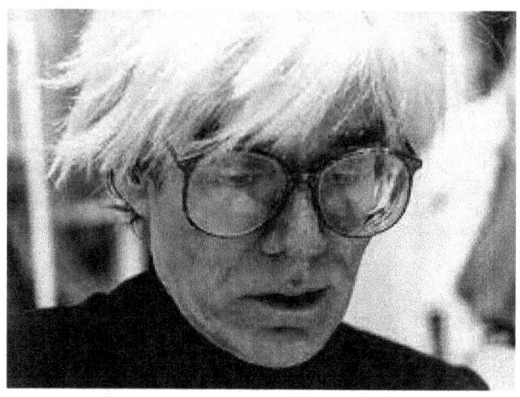

Alias of the American painter , designer , illustrator , sculptor, scriptwriter , actor , director , photographer, producer Andrew Warhola Jr. (1928-1987)

In 1949 graduating moved to New York

In 1968 Valerie Solanas fired at him at the Factory (his studio from 1963 to 1968)

He produced Jean Michel Basquiat and Keith Haring .

In music he was influencial in pop jazz like Velvet Underground & Nico and Curiosity Killed the Cat .

He portrayed the most influential people of his times from sport to cinema to politics. He died after surgery in 1987.

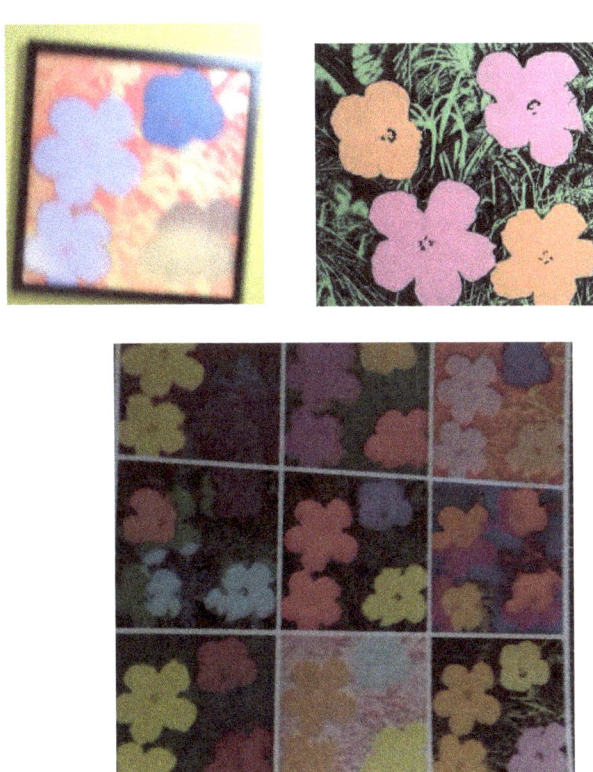

The stain becomes a flowers , the flowers overcoloured in thousand different variations , this is the influence of divisionism .

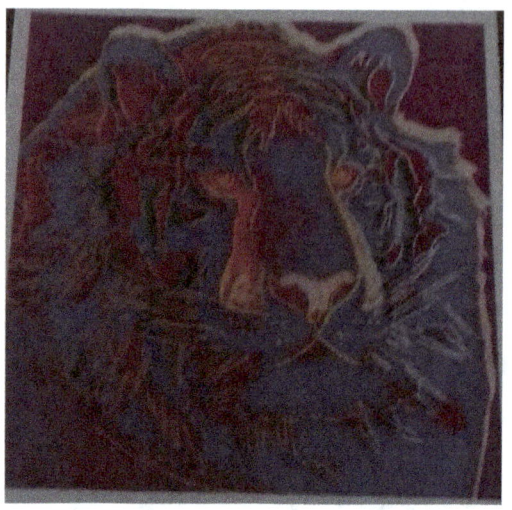

Natural elements are a novelty in Pop Art but the contrast of
the film is exceptional

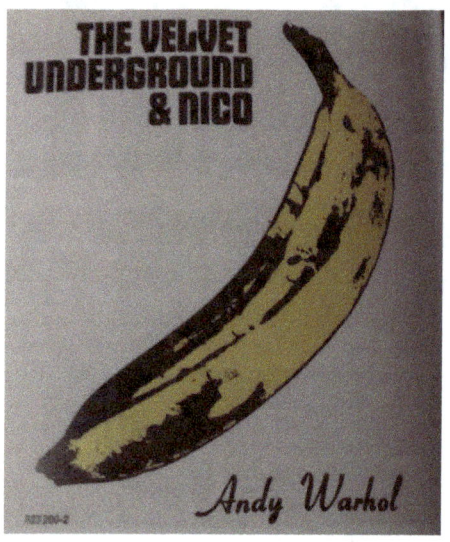

The iconic cover Lp record Of Andy Warhol , the meaning is
ambivalent and ironic as usual.

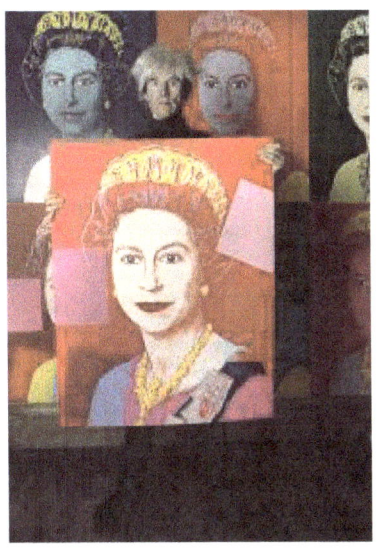

Warhol was keen on living his contemporary history

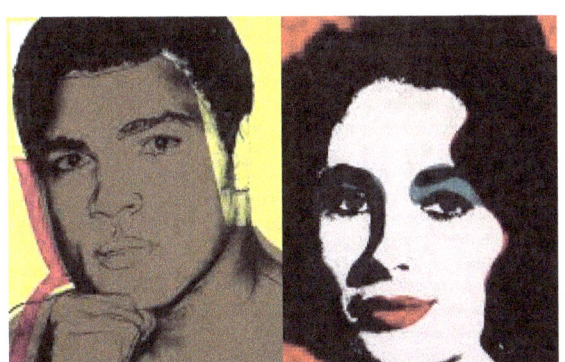

Again the shadows remind us of divisionism .

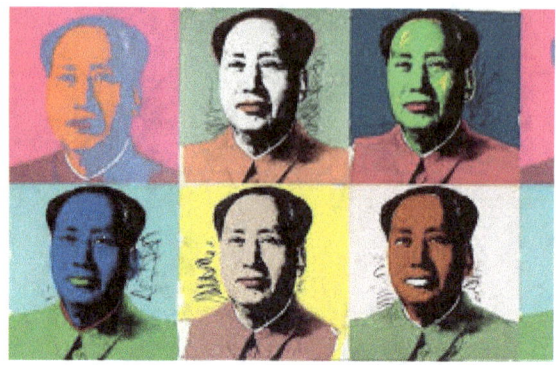

But he also introduced the self

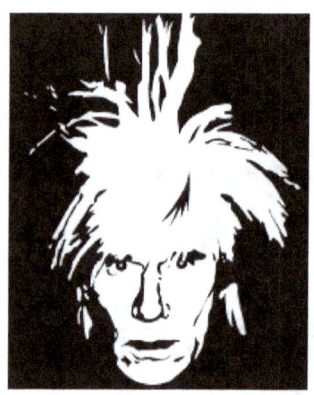
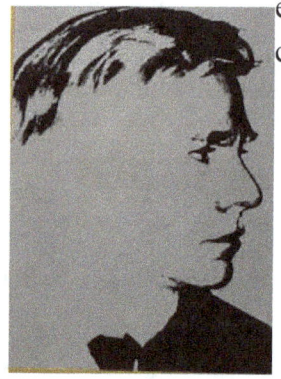

egotistic
cult

Roy Lichtenstein

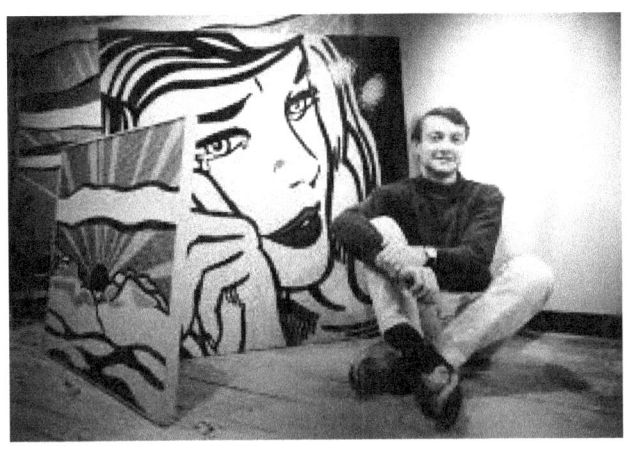

New Yorker painter , sculptor and designer (1923-1997)

He was influenced by Jazz .

In 1943/46 he took part to World War II as technician in the Army

In 1949 graduated and married Isabel Wilson (2 children)

He was influenced by Cubism and Expressionism .

In 1951 first exhibition

From 1957 assistant professor at NY University

In 1962 graffiti for the NY Universal Exposition

From 1972 to 1981 influenced by Futurism and Surrealism

In 1997 died in New York from pneumonia

Roy Lichtenstein`s works

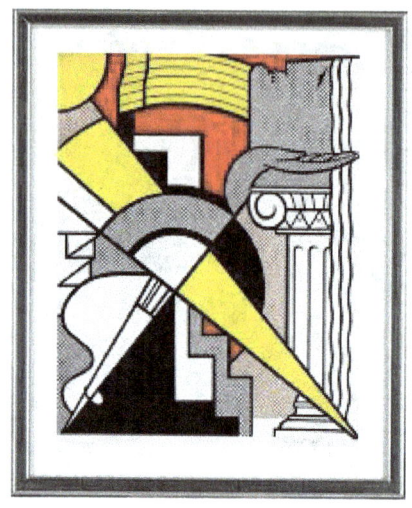

here we can see different influences from Abstractism and the
clock of time , to Metaphysical and the introduction of different
Neoclassical elements from the doric column to the Grecian
silhouette but also the three magical lines , the straight the
circle and the serpentine. Another evident influence is Futurism
with the lightning and the winged wheel . The stairs are an
element both of Dada and of Surrealism . The use of primary
colour remain Piet Mondrian while the column reminds of
Giorgio de Chirico . The yellow red element reminds also of
Nipponism with their red lanterns . There is though a
meditation on war and on the fact that it can restart easily , the
broken lantern shows no safety in life of men.

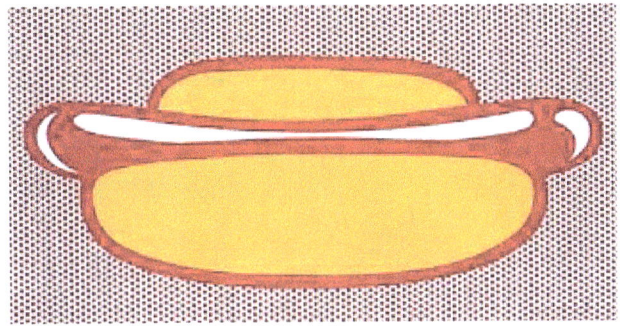

The hot dog is one of the symbols of Junk food in America , the connotation could be ambivalent either reproaching a bad habit but describing a common food with irony or sexual .

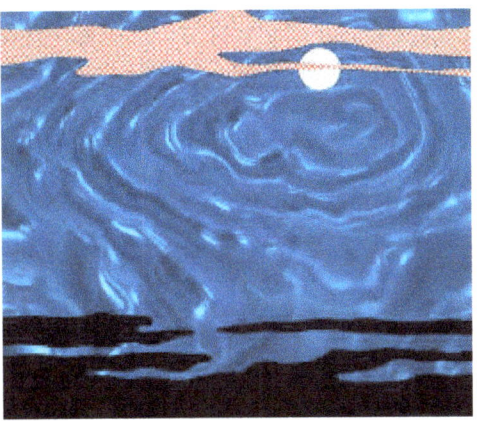

The landscape is reminding of nipponism but the technique of vynil is absolutely innovative .

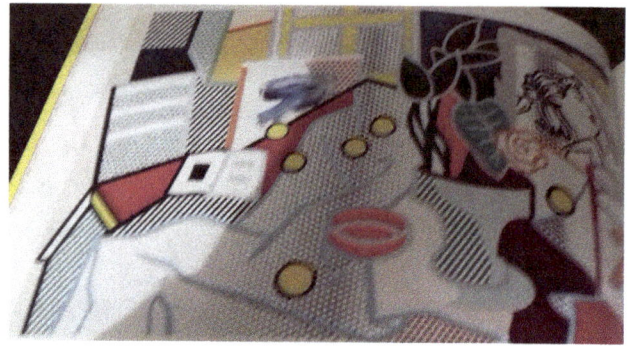

Here we can see all the elements of the different original intuitions of Lichtenstein from the absence of perspective , see the vase to the brush in blue , to the tennis balls and lemons , the interior , the mirrors , the broken image , and the ladies in cartoons . The self portrait either as the observer on the right or the open book with mirror on the left completes the still life that in Lichtenstein is never really still since the technique of graphic design gives movement with the point and double lines and the plants and people who are always part of life.

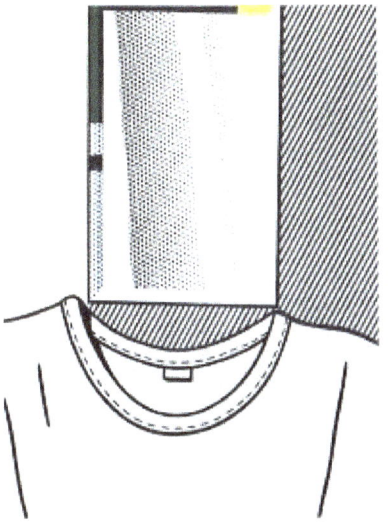

This self portrait is really incredibly existentialist : the object shows the man in his simplicity , like a white t-shirt surmounted by a mirror . The audience is called to measure themselves into the mirror to see if the artist is like them or not . At the same time it is the de-humanized being who is trying to form an identity . One no one or thousand different faces would mirror into the deep introspection of the author.

Robert Rauschenberg

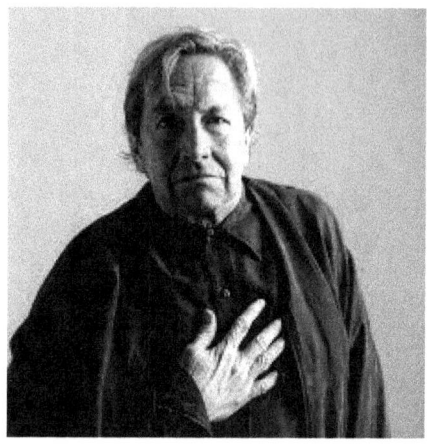

American painter and artist affected by dyslexia (1925/2008)

From 1943 to 46 in the Army as technician

From 1948 studied with Weil at Black Mountain College

In 1950 married Susan Weil paintress (divorced and 1 son in 1953)

Since then bisexual and started homosexual relationship with Darryl Pottorf in 1980s.

In 2008 he died of heart attack after euthanasia .(breather off)

Robert Rauschenberg`s works

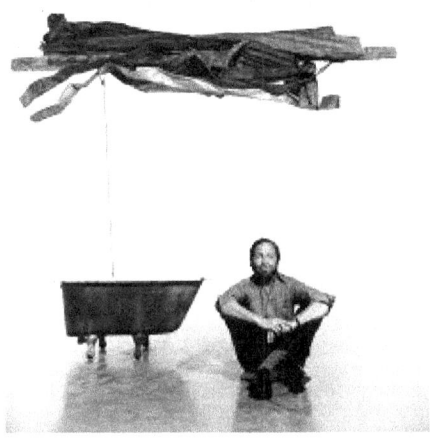

A bath a roof like a grasshopper and the meditation of man .

Would the roof not be a shelter , or poetry and water not be a shelter for man ?

Could man reach movement from his static behaviour and start to act?

Should the performance go on ?

The expression is self satisfied , the grasshopper or cicada can continue in his position to compose meditations or poems .

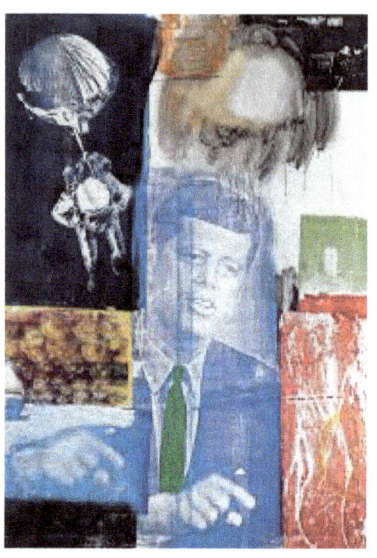

The story of F F Kennedy , the first man on the Moon , the wall of Berlin , Cuba , Vietnam ,and the famous speeches .

The technique is collage, the use of after coloured pictures is innovative , and the contrasts of colours delineating the various scenes of his life .

He calls for the participation of the audience point twice the finger in our direction .

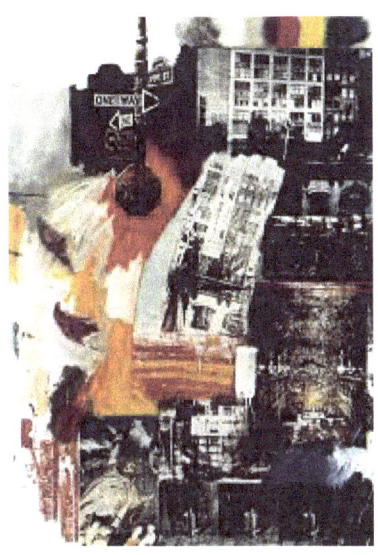

The progress of man is a collage too , in this case it tells us the story of factories and concrete , the urbanization and the city lines.

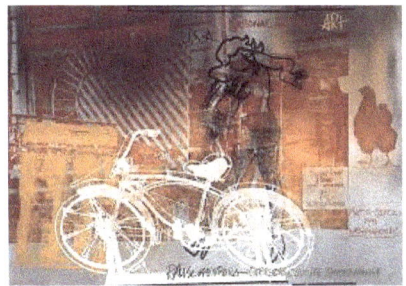

Here we have frottage and collage to remind us of surrealism and the bikes of Dali but also of Dadaism and the ready made by Duchamp . The bike in fact is fixed while the man is moving.

Claes Oldenburg

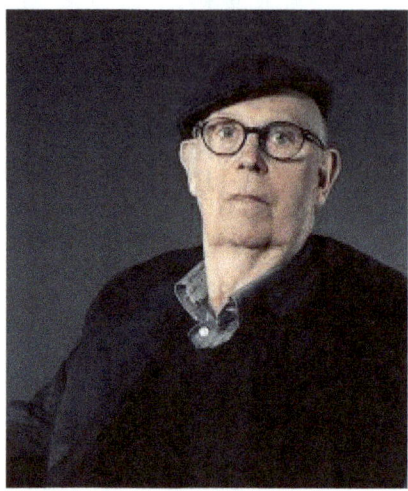

Swedish sculptor and performing artist naturalised American (1929-2022)

In 1936 he moved from Stockholm to Chicago

In 1956 he moved in NY and naturalised

In 1960 he married Pat Muschinski (divorced 1969)

In 1977 he married Coosje van Bruggen the curator of the Stedelijik Museum In Amsterdam and befriended the architect Frank O Gehry

In the 1980s his brother became curator of the MoMa in NY

He died of old age.

Claes Oldenburg works

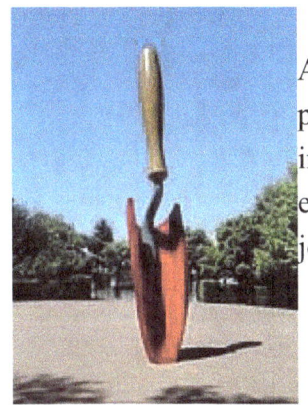

It is the typical object reminding Americans that they are a agricultural population . The giant dimensions are ironising on the fact that in America everything is BIG, as in a bad taste joke.

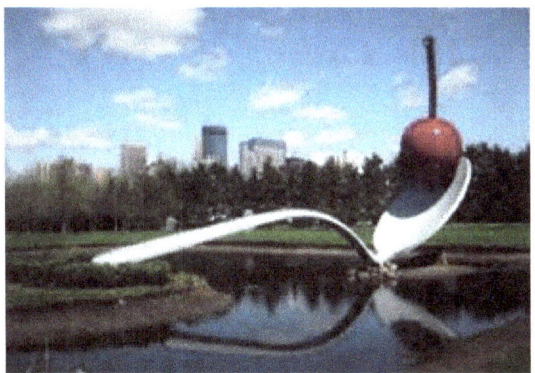

The cherry bridge with the metal spoon , reminds us of the cherry on the top , being the skyline with top skyscrapers and also of a cocktail being it on water . The double scenery natural and artificial are both customized by the spoon, the cherry is natural and the spoon isn`t . The research for moment is evident but we do not know if the cherry will arrive or it will be thrown away as well as the growing building in urban areas.

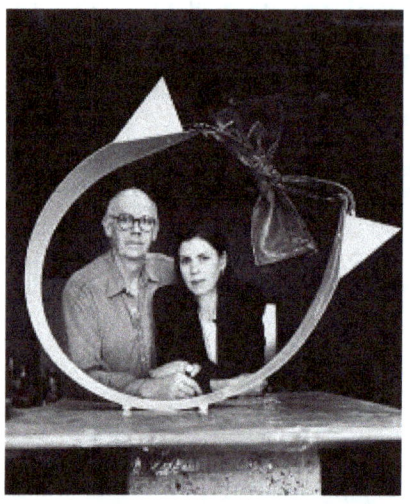

This is a cat with metal and plastic including himself and his wife . And below another artifact with his wife .

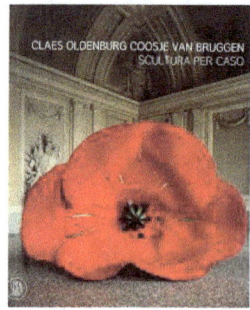

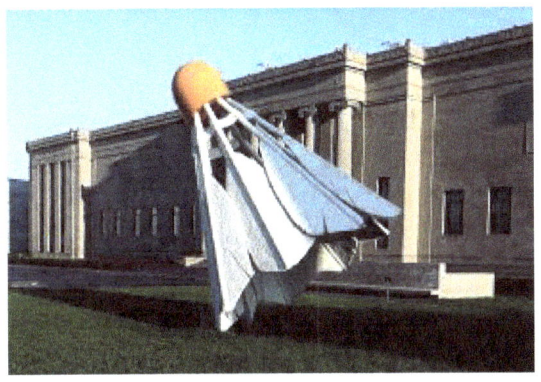

The shuttle of badminton becomes the shuttle rocket symbol of
the space race between America and Russia in front of a
governative building .

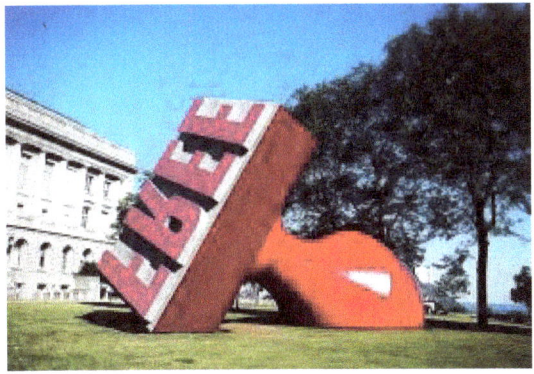

A free print in front of a Museum or University as the culture or the teaching .

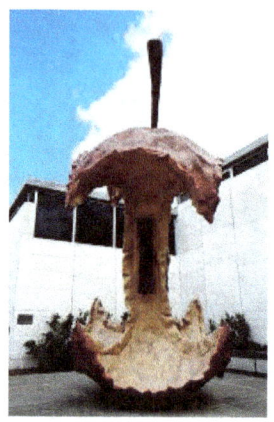

The big apple has been eaten to the remains. The red colour could be also the sign of poison from the fairy tale of Snowwhite which means , mankind has being completely poisoned by bad architecture.

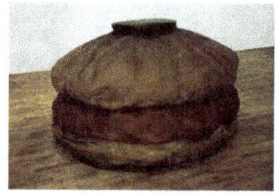

This is called floor burgher , and it is a disgusting object reminding us about junk food .

Robert Indiana

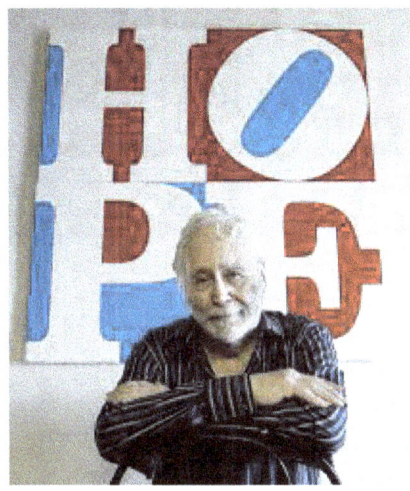

Alias of Robert Clark American artist , sculptor , scenographer and costume maker (1928=2018)

In 1954 he moved to Pop art in New York

invented Sculpted poems with single words

In 1964 he eats a mushroom in the movie by Warhol "Eat"

In the 1970s he devoted to theatre

In 2004 he made Peace Paintings after 9/11

From 1974 he lived on the island of Vinalhaven , Maine.

He died of old age.

Robert Indiana works

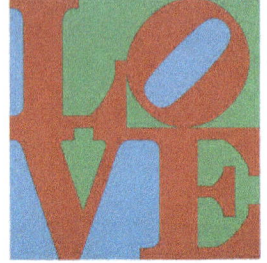
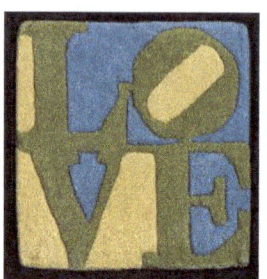

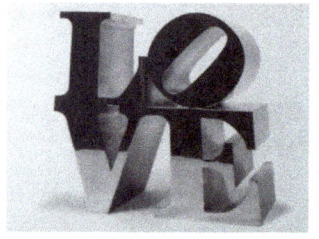
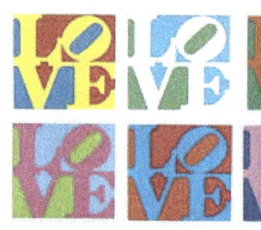

His sculpted poems on different materials have interesting primary full lively colours . You can see the research for moment in the rotation of

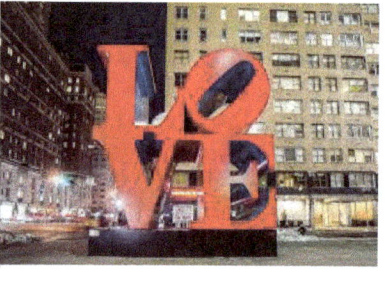

the vowel O and the subliminal use of other symbols like the arrow in V , the balance of justice or a telephone in E and a tap or stitching machine in LO Besides there is a man reading or offering something to drink with the head in O .

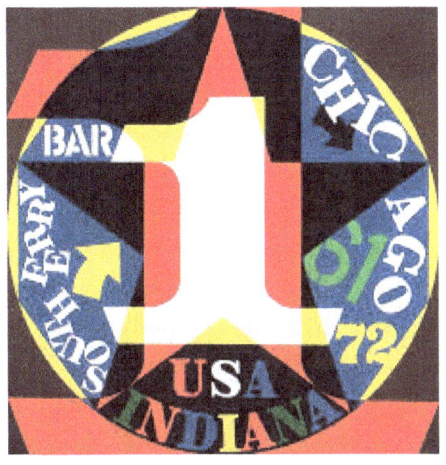

Another sculpted poem is with the use of number and stars ,
and states of the American traditions . Here the use of colour is
different , darker and gloomy , there is the arrow on the left ,
the man in the centre but also a date and Bar and Chic and
South Ferry to Indiana . It reminds of De Pero stilized man and
of theatre , but also of a drunken night somewhere when the
man remains stiff and incapable of moving as in a cross , open
arms , and a patriotic call. A number 1 sailing or practising
archery or firing in Chicago .

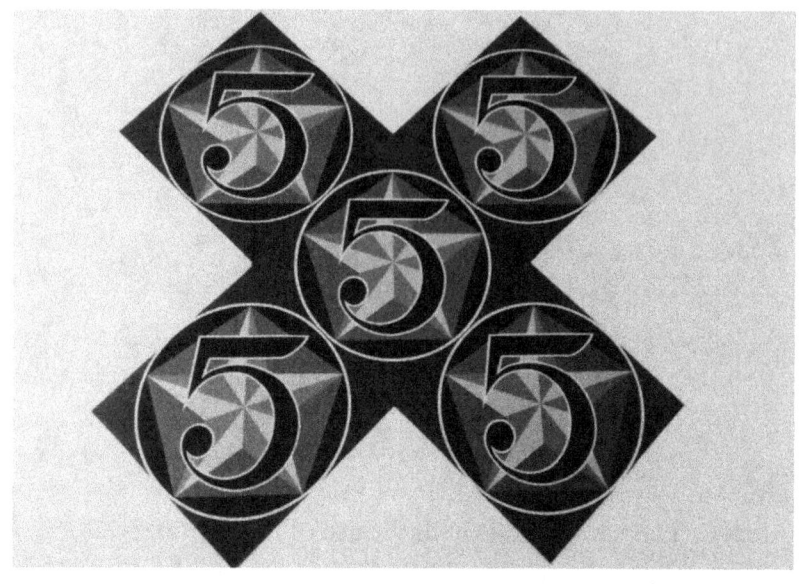

Here the number is 5 , the stars give moment to the cross

It seems a game for children of old times but also a band aid to the five senses , since it is in different shades of gray.

5. Poems influenced by Dada Surrealism and Pop Art

Among others these three movements have influenced contemporary poets after seeing their paintings.

Paul Eluard poems

The Mirror in a moment

The day vanishes ,

it shows to men the unlinked images of appearance ,

it teaches the possibility of enjoyment,

It `s hard as stone

the shapeless stone ,

the stone of movement and sight , and shines such as an armour,

all the masks are shadowed ,

the hand draws a hand to become a hand oneself ,

what was understood does not exist anymore,

the bird is like the wind ,

the sky has its truth--

Man has his reality.

Unknown was my favourite shape

Unknown was my favourite shape ,

the one who lifted me from being a man ,

and I see it and I loose it and I bear ,

my pain , as a little pool of water in the sun.

You cannot know me

You cannot know me better than you know me

Your eyes in which we sleep

both

has given birth to me as a man A better destiny of the world
nights

Your eyes in which I travel has given to the journey

a meaning far from the world

In your eyes which reveal our never ending solitude there is not
what I thought there would be

You cannot know you better Than I know you.

**The necessities of life and the consequences of the dreams
1921 Model**

So many lights,

so many hands and faces,

so many days and nights,

such as the wings of birds !

Destined ,

man , alone , to find everything .

Enter.

Horizons are in scene.

Exit .

Falling of light over a dome

a desert

a star during the day

only for some days.

Guillaume Apollinaire Calligrammes

```
              S
              A
             LUT
              M
            O   N
            D   E
            DONT
            JE SUIS·
            LA LAN
           GUE  É
          LOQUEN
        TE  QUESA
        B O U C H E
         O   PARIS
        TIRE  ET  TIRERA
       T O U        JOURS
      AUX            A  L·
     LEM               ANDS
```

Hello world

where I am the language so eloquent as its mouth

O Paris

you are yielding and will yield to the Germans.

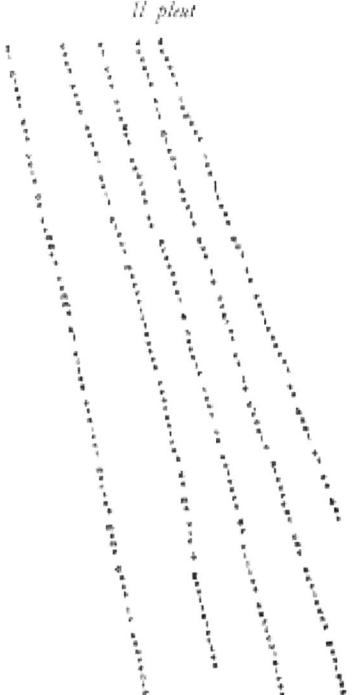

It rains / It cries

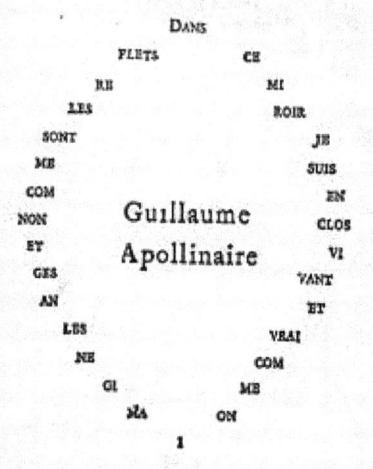

The mirror

I am included in this mirror

living and true like the wings of angels

and naked as are the reflects.

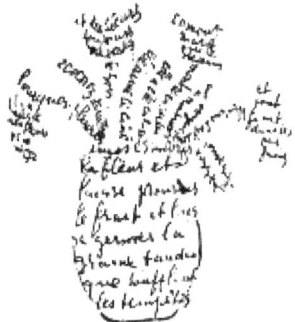

The flowers

Jacques Prevert

From Paroles

Chanson

That day we were us

we are every day

my friend

we are all life long

my love

we love each other and we live

we live and we love each other

and we do not know what life is

and we do not know what day is

and we do not know what love is.

Paris at night

Three matchsticks one by one lighted in the night

the first to see your full face

the second to see your eyes

the third to see your lips

and darkness to remind me of all these

and to hold you in my arms .

The broken mirror

The little man was singing

the little man was dancing over my head

the little man of youth has broken his shoe string

they broke suddenly in the middle of the feast.

In the desert of my mind

I heard his happy voice

His happy and fragile voice

desolate and childish

coming from afar and calling upon me

and he put my hand upon my heart

where remained bloodily the seven chips of the mirror of his
star smiling .

The Beat Generation poems

Gregory Corso from Mindfield

The love of two seasons

When once in wildhood times

I`d aerial laughter my mischief

When once she opened her arms

and held me with excited tenderness

I laughed

she laughed

Our passion transcended

What in seriousness repelled us

and she bid me close my eyes

and behold some dreadful magnificence

Running ice

cold pulse

Memories of ice day ice night

she told me goodbye forever

a month later

a no return address letter came

"I`ve a snow owl and it loves you it loves you"

Jack Kerouac

I clearly saw

21. I clearly saw

I

  clearly

     saw

       the skeleton underneath

all

  this

     show

       of personality

what

  is

   left

    of man and all his pride

but bones ?

And all his lost snacks o` nights –

  and the bathtubs of liquor

thru his gullet

— bones — He mopes

in the grave ,

facial features

changed by worms

*

*

*

*

from him

is heard

no more

*

*

*

*

Life is sick

dogs cough

bees sail

birds hack

trees saw

woods cry

men die

ticks try

books lie

ants fly

Goodbye

***

Lawrence Ferlinghetti

Kafka Castle

Kafka's Castle stands above the world

like a last bastille

of the Mystery of Existence

its blind approaches baffle us

steep paths

plunge nowhere from it

roads radiate into air

like the labyrinth wires

of a telephone central

thru which all calls are

infinitely untraceable

up there

it is heavenly weather

souls dance undressed

together

and like loiterers

on the fringes of a fair

we ogle the unobtainable

imagined mystery

Yet away around on the far side

like the stage door of a circus tent

is a wide wide vent in the battlements

where even elephants

waltz thru

Lawrence Ferlinghetti

In a surrealist yeat

 In a surrealistic year
of sandwichmen and sunbathers

dead sunflowers and live telephones

house-broken politicos with party whips

performed as usual

in the rings of their sawdust circuses

where tumblers and human cannonballs

filled the air like cries

when some cool clown

pressed an inedible mushroom button

and an inaudible Sunday bomb

fell down

catching the president at his prayers

on the 19th green

O it was a spring

of fur leaves and cobalt flowers

when cadillacs fell thru the trees like rain

drowning the meadows with madness

while out of every imitation cloud

dropped myriad wingless crowds

of nutless nagasaki survivors

and lost teacups

full of our ashes

floated by

Lawrence Ferlinghetti

The world is a beautiful place

Th e world is a beautiful place

to be born into

If you don't mind happiness

not always being

to vey much fun

if you don't mind a touch of hell

now and then

just when everything is fine

because even in heaven

they don't sing

all the time

the world is a beautiful place

to be born into

if you don't mind some people dying

all the time

or maybe only starving

some of the time

which isn't half so bad

if it isn't you

Joel Oppenheimer

Leave it to me blues

from the heart of a flower
a stalk emerges ; in each fruit
there are seeds. We turn our
backs on each other so often ,
we destroy any community of
interest , yet our hearts are
seeded with love and care sticks
out of our ears. But there is no
bridge unless it is the wind which
whistles our bare house , tearing
the slipcovers apart and constantly
removing the tablecloth covering
in (the table) like a shroud (the
shroud of what the table could mean
if only we were hungry enough to c

care) and we cut ourselves off
because we discovered each man is
an island , detached , man , the
mainland is flipped over the moon
all I have to depend on is effort ,
and the moon goes round and round
in the evening sky. My sons will
make it if they ever reach age ,
 but how to take care I don't know
it doesn't get better . On the other
hand , even with answers , where
would we be , out in the cold , with
an old torn blanket , and no one
around us to cry

Gregory Corso

This is America

This is America and I'm fun in it

with a wealth of music and lunatics

with a mouth that cannot sing

and I love a woman

and hate the rest and I'll make it

with anything female ten to fifty

and fifty's best

This is America and there's a lot more

fun in it

and lunatics

lots that can`t sing worth a damn

and lots that can

but who gives a damn

I do

In California I sang

my Eastern culture into a dying Mexican`s ear

that couldn`t hear

and he died with a smile on his face

The bastard had three gold teeth

an ounce of tea

a pockeful of peyote

and a fourteen year old wife

Gregory Corso

In the fleeting hand of time

On the steps of the bright madhouse

I hear the bearded bell shaking down the woodlawn

the final knell of my world

I climb and enter a firey gathering of knights

they unaware of my presence lay forth sheepskin plans

and with mailcoated fingers trace my arrival

back back back when on the black steps of Nero lyre Rome I stood

in my arms the wailing philosopher

the final call of mad history

Now my presence is known

my arrival marked by illuminated stains

The great windows of Paradise open

down to radiant dust fall the curtains of Past Time

in fly flocks of multicoloured birds

light winged light O the wonder of light

Time takes me by the hand

born March 26 1930 I am led 100mph o`er the vast market of choice

what to choose? What to choose?

O-- and I leave my orange room of myths

no chance to lock away my toys of Zeus

I choose the room of Bleecker Street

A baby mother stuffs my mouth with a pale Milanese breast

I suck I struggle I cry O Olympian mother

unfamiliar this breast to me

Snows

Decade of icy asphalt doomed horses

Weak dreams Dark corridors of PS 42 Roofs Ratthorated

pigeons

Led 100mph over these all too real Mafia streets

profanely I shed my Hermean wings

O Time be merciful

throw me beneath your humanity of cars

feed me to giant grey skyscrapers

exhaust my heart to your bridges

I discard my lyre of Orphic futility

and for such betrayal I climb these bright mad steps

and enter this room of paradisiacal light

ephemeral

Time

a long long dog having chased its orbited tail

comes grab my hand

and leads me into conditional life

Gregory Corso

Paris

Childcity, Aprilcity,

spirits of angels crouched in doorways,

poets, worms in hair , beautiful Baudelaire

Artaud , Rimbaud , Apollinaire

Look to the nightcity--

Informers and concierges

Montparnassian woe , deathical Notre Dame

to the nightcircle look , dome heirloomed,

Hugo and Zola together entombed

Harlequin deathtrap

Seine generates ominous mud

Eiffel looks down – sees the Apocalyptical ant crawl

New Yorkless city ,

City of the Germans dead and gone ,

Dollhouse of Mama War.

Allen Ginsberg

Now and forever

I'll settle for Immortality
not thru the body
not thru the eyes
star-spangled high mountains
waning moon over Aspen peaks
but thru words , thru the breath
of long sentences
loves I have heart beating
still
inspiration continuous , exhalation of
cadenced affection
These immortal survive America
survive the fall of States
departure of my body
mouth dumb dust
this verse broadcasts desire
accomplishment of Desire
Now and forever boys can read
girls dream , old men cry
old women sigh
youth still come

Satisfaction by Rolling Stones

I can't get no satisfaction
I can't get no satisfaction
'Cause I try, and I try, and I try, and I try
I can't get no, I can't get no

When I'm driving in my car
When a man come on the radio
He's telling me more and more
About some useless information
Supposed to fire my imagination

I can't get no, oh, no, no, no, hey, hey, hey
That's what I say
I can't get no satisfaction
I can't get no satisfaction
'Cause I try, and I try, and I try, and I try
I can't get no, I can't get no

When I'm watchin' my TV
And a man comes on and tells me
How white my shirts can be
But, he can't be a man 'cause he doesn't smoke
The same cigarettes as me

I can't get no, oh, no, no, no, hey, hey, hey
That's what I say
I can't get no satisfaction
I can't get no girl reaction
'Cause I try, and I try, and I try, and I try
I can't get no, I can't get no

When I'm ridin' 'round the world
And I'm doin' this and I'm signin' that
And I'm tryin' to make some girl, who tells me
Baby, better come back maybe next week
Can't you see I'm on a losing streak?
I can't get no, oh, no, no, no, hey, hey, hey
That's what I say
I can't get no, I can't get no
I can't get no satisfaction, no satisfaction
No satisfaction, no satisfaction
I can't get no

Sunday Morning by Velvet Underground and Nico

Sunday morning, brings the dawn in
It's just a restless feeling by my side
Early dawning, Sunday morning
It's just the wasted years so close behind

Watch out, the world's behind you
There's always someone around you who will call
It's nothing at all

Sunday morning and I'm falling
I've got a feeling I don't want to know
Early dawning, Sunday morning
It's all the streets you crossed, not so long ago

Watch out, the world's behind you
There's always someone around you who will call
It's nothing at all

Watch out, the world's behind you
There's always someone around you who will call
It's nothing at all

Sunday morning

Misfits by Curiosity Killed the Cat

Sensitive child keep running wild in a confined space
You're not to blame 'cause you're not the same
Get on the case crazy sheep, you are the odd one out

Crazy sheep let them know what you're all about
Misfit freak that's on the street
Well, I can see the sorrow in your eyes

How long? how low?
How high can you go?
There'll be a bind for every kind, you'll see

Sensitive child your threat is so mild, it worries me
Build yourself some protection to avoid the injection
Then you can be happy

Crazy sheep you are the odd on out
Crazy sheep let them know what you're all about

Misfit freak that's on the street
Now I can see the sorrow in your eyes

Set your mode to emotion, your secret potion
Designed to satisfy your soul
And underneath your broken dreams
You need to satisfy your soul

Misfit freak that's on the street
Now I can see the sorrow in your eyes

Too fat, too thin, you lose or you win
This may come as some surprise
Too tall, too short, too loose or too taut
There'll be a bind for every kind

Misfit freak that's on the street
Now I can see the sorrow in your eyes

Too fat, too thin, you lose or you win
You've got to satisfy your soul
And underneath your broken dreams
You need to satisfy your soul

Bibliography

Open sources like wikipedia , exhibitions , and the encyclopedia Art anthology vol 4,5 6 edited by Zanichelli